THE
CHALLENGE
— OF —
GOLF

THE CHALLENGE
OF
GOLF

CHRIS PLUMRIDGE

—— INTRODUCTION BY ——

SEVE BALLESTEROS

St Michael

This edition published for
Marks & Spencer plc in 1987
by Century Benham Ltd, Brookmount House,
62–65 Chandos Place, London WC2N 4NW

ISBN 0 7126 2661 1

Produced by Lennard Books Ltd
Mackerye End, Harpenden, Herts AL5 5DR

Editor Michael Leitch
Designed by Pocknell & Co
Production Reynolds Clark Associates Ltd
Photoset by Jigsaw Graphics
Printed and bound in Yugoslavia

For Vanessa

COVER PHOTOGRAPHS

FRONT
Main photograph
Jack Nicklaus plays to the green during the 1986
World Match-Play at Wentworth.
Inset Seve Ballesteros gets out of trouble
during the 1985 Ryder Cup at The Belfry.

BACK
Bobby Clampett in some difficulty during the 1983 Open at
Royal Birkdale.

CONTENTS

Introduction by Severiano Ballesteros
7

CHAPTER ONE
St Andrews — The Home of Golf
9

CHAPTER TWO
Cleeks and Featheries: Golf Equipment and How it Developed
17

CHAPTER THREE
Golf's Greatest Challenges
31

CHAPTER FOUR
The Majors and the World Match–Play
61

CHAPTER FIVE
Great Advice
99

CHAPTER SIX
The Story of Women's Golf
104

CHAPTER SEVEN
The Seniors
112

CHAPTER EIGHT
Golfing Celebrities
116

CHAPTER NINE
Famous Careers
122

Index/Acknowledgements
173

INTRODUCTION

When I first started to play golf as a boy in
Pedreña, I had just one club. For me then,
the challenge was to discover what I
could do with the golf ball using that
single club. It was a terrific education. By
experimenting I learned to hit the ball
many different ways – high, low, hooked or
sliced – and through this I also learned the
feel of the ball off the clubface. There were
other challenges too. These were
competing with the other boys who were
also caddies at Pedreña. We would go down
to the beach and make a course because we
were not allowed on the golf course.
Playing for more pesetas than I could afford
to lose made me try harder and I think,
maybe, I never lost.

    Challenging the course and
competing against other players are the
two things that make golf the best of all
games. Whether you are playing in the
Open Championship or in a medal at your
home club, these two things remain
constant. I think this book combines the
two things in a very beautiful way. The
man who wrote it, Chris Plumridge, is
always watching me in the tournaments
and knows and loves the game, and the
photographs also show great affection for
golf.

    Enjoy this book and enjoy your
golf. Because every day on the course, the
challenge is different.

ST ANDREWS – THE HOME OF GOLF

For golfers from all over the world, a visit to St Andrews is considered mandatory if their golfing education is to be complete. This small Fifeshire town is regarded as the place where man's love affair with club and ball was first consummated, so initiating the history, legend and myth which pervade every corner of the 'auld grey toon' and its golf courses.

In truth, St Andrews cannot really lay claim to being the birthplace of the game in spite of numerous public relations exercises to prove otherwise. A noted historian, Professor Douglas Young, actually went as far as to ascertain that golf was invented by a St Andrews University student but it is far more likely that the concept of hitting a ball over open countryside to a defined target was imported from Holland. The Dutch game of *spel metten colve* (game played with a club) was well established in the 13th century and the name gradually evolved to *kolf*. This was a cross-country game played over a series of separate areas using wooden balls and implements closely resembling early golf clubs.

Early *kolf* was played towards large targets, such as church doors, but as the skill of the participants increased then these targets were replaced by poles. The poles were ornately carved and soon became desirable targets for thieves who removed them. Each theft was marked by a hole in the ground, which the players then adopted as the final resting-place for the ball. Early Flemish paintings actually depict *kolf* being played to a hole.

Much of this evidence is circumstantial but it is far more firmly based than the picturesque idea of old Scottish farmers rolling an acorn into a rabbit-scrape with a walking stick or crook. Furthermore, in the 15th century St Andrews was one of the most important ports north of the Forth and regular trade took place between the harbour and the Low Countries. The Scottish army also made forays to the Continent and these interchanges of trade and warfare resulted in *kolf* taking root along that strip of land which linked the sea to the mainland. One can imagine the Dutch merchants of the day arriving in St Andrews, walking from the harbour in the River Eden estuary to the town and recognizing that the land they were passing was ideally suited to their pastime.

1384. Golf or Bandy-ball. One of the earliest references to golf.

Mercifully, this strip of land was useless for anything save as a recreation area for the locals and a place for washerwomen to dry clothes on the whin (furze) bushes, the latter being a right which still exists to this day although one cannot imagine it being exercised in the middle of the Open Championship! The earliest documentation of golf in St Andrews is a licence granted in 1552 to the inhabitants allowing them to use the common links 'to play at golf, futball, schuting, at all gamis with all uther maner of pastime, as ever thai pleis'. However, it is well known that an earlier reference to the game in Scotland occurred when James II in 1457 issued a proclamation that 'the futball and the golfe be utterly cryit downe and not usit' since these activities interfered with archery practice. (The connection between golf and archery is explored more fully elsewhere.) To continue in the vernacular vein, it is also recorded that the Edinburgh town council of 1592 issued a ban on 'ony pastymes or gammis within or without the toun upoun the Sabboth day, sic as Gof', and transgressors were punished with a 40 shilling fine if caught.

From these documents and other historical evidence, such as the indictment of Mary Queen of Scots for playing golf a few days after the death of her husband, Lord Darnley, it is clear that golf was being played in Scotland with some enthusiasm. However, any standardization of the game to a form that would be recognizable today was a long time in coming. Indeed, it took close on two hundred years of knocking a ball about on that common links land before anybody decided to bring about any kind of order. Other than a mention in the court records of Kelso that one Thomas Chatto was killed by a blow from a golf club, wielded by a man playing golf in a churchyard, we have to alight from the time capsule on 14 May 1754 to sit in on the first Rules

The whin and scrub of St Andrews, viewed from the 3rd tee.

Committee meeting of 'The Society of St Andrews Golfers'. The meeting was chaired by Charles, 5th Earl of Elgin and 9th Earl of Kincardine, and was attended by 21 other noblemen and gentry for the purpose of establishing and drafting certain 'Articles and Laws pertaining to the healthful exercise of the Golf'. These 22 men had little idea of what they were starting but all of them were keen golfers and some were also proficient archers.

Even the Rules of the game at that time were not formulated by St Andreans; 11 years earlier, the Company of Edinburgh Golfers, later the Honourable Company of Edinburgh Golfers, who played on the Links of Leith, had come up with 13 rules and these were adopted by St Andrews as follows:

'1. You must tee your Ball within a Club Length of the hole.

2. Your tee must be upon the Ground.

3. You are not to Change the Ball which you Strike off the Tee.

your Adversary's Ball, not lying in your way to the hole.

8. If you should lose your Ball, by its being taken up, or any other way You are to go back to the Spot where you Struck last, and drop another ball, and Allow your Adversary a stroke for the Misfortune.

9. No Man at holeing his Ball, is to be Allowed to Mark his way to the Hole with his Club or anything else.

10. If a Ball be Stop'd by any person, Horse, Dog or any thing else, the Ball so Stop'd Must be played where it lyes.

11. If you draw your Club, in Order to Strike, and proceed so far in the Stroke as to be bringing down your Club; if then your Club shall break, in any way, it is to be counted a Stroke.

12. He, Whose Ball lyes furthest from the Hole is Obliged to play first.

13. Neither Trench, Ditch, or Dyke made for the preservation of the Links, Nor the Scholars Holes or the Soldiers Lines, shall

An early game of golf in Edinburgh during the 18th century.

4. You are not to Remove Stones, Bones or any Break Club for the Sake of playing your Ball Except upon the fair Green and that only within a Club Length of your Ball.

5. If your Ball come among Water, or any Watery filth, You are at Liberty to take Your Ball, and throwing it behind the hazard 6 yards at least. You may play it with any Club, and allow your Adversary a Stroke, for so getting out your Ball.

6. If your Balls be found anywhere touching one another, You are to lift the first Ball, till You play the last.

7. At holeing, You are to play your Ball honestly for the Hole, and not play upon

be accounted a Hazard, But the Ball is to be taken out, Teed and played with any Iron Club.'

Many modern-day golfers would prefer that these original 13 Rules had remained untouched, except for a little updating in the style and grammar, for they have spawned 41 Rules of Golf, umpteen sub-sections and paragraphs and countless definitions which are designed to cover every contingency but actually create massive confusion simply because today's golfers cannot be bothered to read them all.

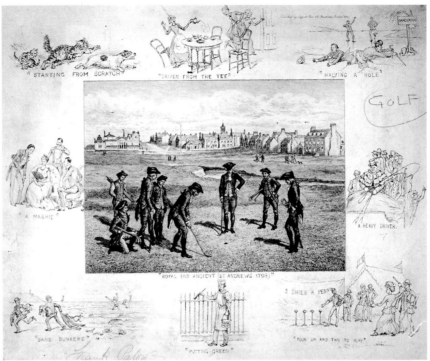

Golfers on the links at
St Andrews in 1798.

Be that as it may, this meeting in May 1754 gave some official status to the St Andrews golfers, and on that same day the founder members subscribed to a silver club for competition, the winner to attach to it a silver ball with his name engraved on it. The first winner was Bailie William Landale, a merchant in the town, who then became the first Captain of the Society.

Regular meetings were held in Glass's Inn and later in the Union Parlour, where in 1835 the Union Club was founded for the combined benefit of the St Andrews Archers Club and the Golf Club. It was in 1834 that the club applied to the reigning monarch, King William IV, for permission to take the name of the Royal and Ancient Golf Club. This was granted and in 1837 the King William IV Gold Medal was obtained for play as the scratch prize in the club's Autumn Meeting; in the previous year the Queen Adelaide Gold Medal had been obtained to be worn by each Captain at public functions during the term of his office.

By now St Andrews had established itself as the centre of the game due to the excellence of the Old Course

and the fact that the Honourable Company of Edinburgh Golfers had lost ground, both literally and metaphorically, by having to change its site. In 1853 it was decided at St Andrews that permanent premises should be built, and a year later the Royal and Ancient Clubhouse was opened.

More and more people now turned to the club for guidance on the game and interpretations of the rules, and in 1860 it was one of the clubs invited to send a pair of players to compete in the first Open Championship at Prestwick, and to be represented on the committee which formed the Championship. The ultimate breakthrough for the club, so far as the government of the game is concerned, came in 1897 when, having been approached by several other leading clubs, the Royal and Ancient agreed to become the governing authority on the Rules of Golf.

In relation to its early beginnings, the rise of the Royal and Ancient has been positively meteoric. Following that fateful day in 1897, other countries sought guidance from the club and now every country outside North

The card room in the
R & A clubhouse.

The main club room at the
R & A looking out over the
1st and 18th holes.

stands as the premier international title,
attracting the finest players in the world
who relish the challenge of competing
over a regular rota of seaside links courses.
The staging of the Open, as it is
universally called, is now a million-pound
operation involving a great many
commercial interests. The greater part of
its growth took place under the guiding
hand of Keith Mackenzie, Secretary to the
club for 17 years (1967–84) who worked
tirelessly to promote the image of the
Championship abroad, particularly in
America where, despite the presence of
Arnold Palmer in the 1960 Open, the
event had a reputation for being an
anachronistic throwback to a bygone era
with prize-money to match.

America, where the rules are governed by
the United States Golf Assocation, plays
the game under R & A Rules. The R & A
and the USGA work in harmony on the
Rules and meet regularly to discuss and
update where necessary.

The club now has a membership
approaching 2,000 and from this various
sub-committees are formed to handle
different areas of the game, some dealing
with questions about rules, others with
requests to approve implements and balls,
while the club also supplies selection
committees for international matches such
as the Walker Cup and the Eisenhower
Trophy. It is in the area of championship
golf that the R & A has exercised the most
influence. Before World War I, a small
group of clubs had been responsible for
running the Open and Amateur
Championships but in 1919 it was agreed
that the R & A should assume total
responsibility for the two. A
championship committee was formed, and
to its list of events were later added the
Boys' Championship, in 1949, the Youths'
Championship in 1963, and the Seniors'
in 1970.

The Open Championship now

Keith Mackenzie at Royal
Birkdale in 1983, his last
year as Secretary of the
R & A.

An aerial view of the stands and tented village during the 1984 Open.

That is hardly the case now as prize-money is well in excess of £600,000 and still rising with perhaps the Championship's finest hour occurring in 1984 at St Andrews when record crowds totalling nearly 200,000 attended during the week. A far cry indeed from that May day of 1754 when 22 men sat down and decided to form a golf club.

Unlike many other clubs, the R & A does not own any of the four courses in St Andrews, but administers and maintains them through a joint links trust with the town council. Of these four courses, the Old, the Jubilee, the New and the Eden, the Old remains the original masterpiece, fashioned by Nature with a few additions by beast and man. It stands as a prototype for courses all over the world and its influence on golf course architecture is without parallel.

At first sight, the Old Course appears nondescript, a flat, featureless stretch of land dotted with clumps of gorse, hardly in keeping with its reputation. To play the Old Course however, is to come to terms with yourself as a golfer. It cannot be bludgeoned into submission and, like any faithful aged retainer, it will only respond to your bidding through coaxing combined with an element of firmness. Certainly, the Old Course lacks the one quality so sought after by the modern professional – fairness. There are few clearly defined targets, there are a host of humps and hollows to divert the ball, there are numerous concealed bunkers, some so small that there is, as Bernard Darwin once wrote, 'only room for one angry man and his niblick', and finally, in a twist of which Torquemada would have been proud, there are the enormous double greens.

The evolution of these unique greens began around 1840. Until then,

the strip of land shaped like a shepherd's crook was so narrow that there was only room for single greens. As more people took up the game, the club realized the advisability of having separate fairways and greens for the outward and homeward journeys. Two holes were cut in the greens and the fairways were widened. Only four holes have their own single greens and it is due to this arrangement that we have the golfing terms 'out' and 'home'.

It is also due to St Andrews that a round of golf comprises 18 holes. At the outset, the course had 12 holes running out to the River Eden. The golfers set forth from beside the home hole and played out to the end for 11 holes before turning for home, playing the same 11 holes in the reverse direction, thereby completing a round of 22 holes. In 1764, the Royal & Ancient decided that the first four holes should become two, thus also converting the four holes on the way home

into two and reducing the round from 22 holes to 18.

The specific terrors of the 11th, 14th and 17th on the Old Course are dealt with elsewhere; suffice to say here that a myriad of pitfalls wait to ensnare and entrap the unwary golfer as he or she makes the pilgrimage around the world's most famous course. How the golfer reacts to the twin imposters of triumph and disaster can reveal to a keen observer a great deal more about somebody's character than anything said on a psychiatrist's couch.

Modern watering systems and other equipment have removed some of the fire from the Old Course but, given a degree of wind, it can still extract terrible revenge. The history of championships at St Andrews is littered with incidents where players had scorecards bulging with birdies only to have them pilfered by the Old Course's sleight of hand. The current

Drinks at St Andrews 4th or Ginger Beer hole which got its nickname from the refreshment that was sold there.

15

The historic town of
St Andrews.

course record stands at 65, held jointly by Neil Coles and Greg Norman, and the lowest 72-hole total for the Open is 276, set by Severiano Ballesteros in 1984 during a week of balmy weather.

The history of the town of St Andrews is rich and colourful. Formerly the ecclesiastical capital of Scotland and home of that country's oldest university, founded in 1413, its beginnings date back to 747. Here, legend has it, lie some of the bones of St Andrew, the brother of Simon Peter who was crucified on the *Crux decussata* (the X-shaped cross) as he felt he was unworthy to be crucified on the same type of cross as Christ.

Like any self-respecting religious centre, the town has witnessed plunder and pillage, desecration of its cathedral and destruction of its monastery; its clerics have been martyred at the stake and witches drowned. Through its streets wander the ghosts of Mary Queen of Scots, whose parents, James V and Mary of Lorraine, were married in the cathedral in 1538; of the headless Darnley, her murdered husband, and of John Knox, the fire-and-brimstone preacher.

Today's ghosts are much more likely to be seen carrying a hickory-shafted cleek for, to all and sundry, St Andrews means golf. Although the debate still rages as to where the game was actually born, there is no doubt that St Andrews was the cradle. Down the hallowed fairways of the Old Course have passed captains and kings: both George VI and his brother, Edward VIII, are past captains of the R & A, and they march in tandem with the great names of Tom Morris Senior and Junior, Braid, Taylor, Vardon, Hagen, Jones, Cotton, right through to the present era of Nicklaus, Watson, Norman and Ballesteros. All have added wonderfully to the tapestry of St Andrews and perhaps it is fitting that the last word should go to the immortal Bobby Jones who, on the occasion of his receiving the Freedom of the City of St Andrews in 1958, said: 'I could take out of my life everything except my experiences at St Andrews and I'd still have a rich, full life.'

Members enjoy a grandstand view of the closing stages of the 1984 Open.

CLEEKS AND FEATHERIES: GOLF EQUIPMENT AND HOW IT DEVELOPED

The belief that a better game can be bought off the shelf has long been held by golfers, and manufacturers of both golf clubs and balls have not been slow in exploiting this aspect of the golfer's psyche. Row upon row of gleaming weaponry adorns the walls of most professionals' shops, promoted by extensive advertising which proclaims the benefits of space-age technology; place this in your hands, and you will be able to release all your latent energy into a drive of gargantuan proportions. That energy, latent or otherwise, will be focused exclusively on a small, dimpled spheroid which is also promoted as containing enough technology to send a monkey to Saturn and only needs a gentle tap to trigger its rocket-booster mechanism.

This is golf in its modern form. A constant search for greater distance from both club and ball with control and finesse being reduced to mere walk-on parts in the present power-play scenario.

As the 21st century approaches like an express train, it would be a foolish person who thought that golf club and ball development had reached its highest point, for the game has always needed new ideas in this department. Indeed, without this pioneering spirit, the game which took root on the east coast of Scotland would have been abandoned as a worthless pursuit.

Ever since man, or woman for that matter, first took up a stick and took a swish at a stationary object, the desire to launch that object further and higher has been almost overpowering. When the desire was channelled into hitting the object over a designated stretch of land to a defined target, then it rapidly became clear what was most efficient for doing the hitting and what was most efficient for receiving the hit.

GOLF BALL DEVELOPMENT

Early pictorial evidence, particularly Flemish paintings, shows *kolf* being played on frozen canals with a large ball, probably constructed from boxwood, and with a club resembling an ice-hockey stick. Since the ball was hard and unyielding, the club possessed a large, long-nosed head to provide the player with sufficient mass at impact with the ball. One can imagine that such an implement would be good for sending the ball skimming across the ice. Once the game took place on land, however, the results would not be so pleasing since the size and weight of the ball would make it difficult to get it airborne. For that reason a lighter, smaller ball had to be found. An early solution was the feather-stuffed ball, or featherie, which was first mentioned on record in 1620 but had probably been in existence some time before that.

Manufacture of the featherie was a tedious business and an expert could

The evolution of the golf ball. From back to front: featherie, guttie, chisel-marked guttie, two examples of early moulded surface patterns, the bramble pattern, the lattice or mesh pattern, an early dimpled ball, a traditional Dunlop 65 and the same company's DDH dimple pattern.

only produce four or five a day. Each ball was hand-made by creating a spherical bag from strips of cowhide stitched together; the bag was then filled with feathers stuffed in through a gap left for this purpose. The feathers, as many as would fill a top hat, were first boiled to break down and soften the quills; after they had been packed into the bag, the aperture was sewn up. The ball was hammered all over to make it as round as possible, and finally painted. Featherie ball-making became a serious industry in Scotland; the various manufacturers each had their individual methods and styles of production, and this meant there was little standardization, the size and weight of each ball varying according to the amount and thickness of the leather used. Nowadays, a featherie ball, particularly those made by the firm of W. & J. Gourlay of Musselburgh, are much prized as collector's items, and a ball in reasonable condition can fetch up to £1,000 at auction.

The featherie dominated the game of golf for some 400 years until the middle of the 19th century despite possessing a number of drawbacks. Chief among these was that it was rarely a true sphere and thus was unpredictable in flight and even more unpredictable along the ground. Its casualty rate was extremely high in wet weather when the casing and innards became sodden and were then easy prey for an ill-timed approach with an iron club. Because of this, and also because of the labourious manufacturing process, featheries were expensive and only well-to-do golfers could afford them. This had the effect of creating the image of golf as a rich man's game, a pastime not for the masses. It is only recently that this image has been dispelled.

The next significant change in golf-ball manufacture occurred in 1848 with the arrival of the gutta-percha ball, or guttie. The properties of this material were first recognized by Mr William Montgomerie, surgeon to the East India Company in Malaya. He noted that the locals used the sap from gum trees to fashion the handles of daggers and knives,

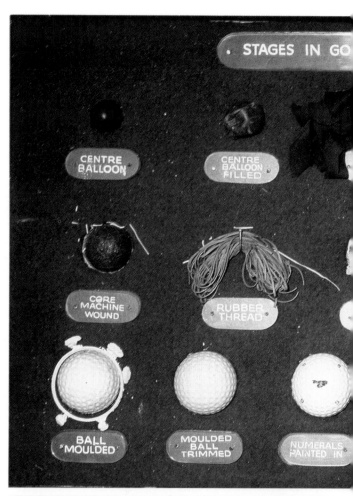

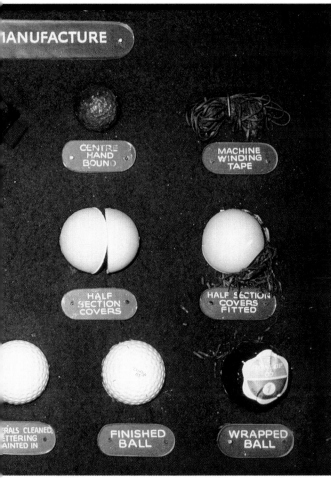

MANUFACTURE

CENTRE HAND BOUND

MACHINE WINDING TAPE

HALF SECTION COVERS

HALF SECTION COVERS FITTED

RALS CLEANED, TTERING AINTED IN

FINISHED BALL

WRAPPED BALL

Above Golf-ball manufacture explained in a showcase at the R & A museum.

Left An old iron mould for making golf balls.

indentations on the ball increased, so it flew more satisfactorily.

The tide of progress could not be stemmed and the featherie quickly became obsolete. Gutties were now nicked and indented before play; ball production increased and the costs came down. The final death-knell for the featherie was sounded when the guttie was produced in an iron mould with the indentations on the inside which did away with the manual process of producing them with a pointed hammer. Golfers now had a ball that was consistent in flight and roll, was relatively inexpensive and which could also be repaired by simply placing it in hot water and then dropping it back into the mould. The first great golf explosion was now underway.

Compared with that of the featherie, the guttie's reign was brief. In 1902 there appeared a ball which completely revolutionized the game. This was the rubber-cored ball or 'Haskell', named after its creator, Coburn Haskell of Cleveland, Ohio. Haskell latched onto the idea of wrapping thin rubber strips round an elastic core under tension. He and his friend, Bertram Work, submitted specifications to the US Patent Office in 1898 and after a few modifications the Goodrich Rubber Company of Akron, Ohio, where Haskell had first seen the rubber strips, went into production. The ball still had a gutta-percha cover but in all other respects was totally different. No more were golfers subject to the dull response of the guttie which, when topped, hardly went anywhere. Instead, the new ball bounded along even when poorly struck. There were those people who regarded the Haskell with contempt, believing it gave its users an unfair advantage. They referred to it as a 'Bounding Billy' and to those who used it as 'bounders' – a name which is still used to describe people who don't quite play the game.

The new ball's first success came in 1901 when Walter J. Travis won the US Amateur Championship using it, and the following year it invaded Britain. While practising for the 1902 Open Championship, Alexander 'Sandy' Herd

and that this substance could readily be softened by immersion in hot water. It was then but a short step to take the gutta-percha and roll it on a flat board until it assumed a spherical shape, and was then left to harden.

Great was the consternation when the guttie ball first arrived in Scotland. The featherie ball-makers dismissed it as a seven-day wonder and took particular delight when the first attempts to get the new ball airborne resulted in it diving to the ground like a wounded grouse. This, however, was purely a question of aerodynamics since the early gutties were completely smooth and lacked any means of cleaving a path through the air. The problem was solved by accident when players who persisted with the guttie found that, as the round progressed and the number of nicks and

was persuaded to try one, and he went out and won the title over four rounds at Hoylake, using, it is alleged, the same ball throughout.

The Haskell was the forerunner of the modern golf ball. Other substances were used for the cover, mainly balata, but the principle of winding rubber under tension around a core remained. It was a principle which enabled manufacturers to create highly resilient balls which could travel prodigious distances and it soon became evident that something had to be done if the game was to retain its elements of skill and control.

In 1912, a meeting between the golf ball manufacturers and the Royal and Ancient achieved some sort of voluntary restriction on the initial velocity of the ball but there was still no standardization of size or weight. Heavy balls could be purchased as well as lighter ones, known as 'floaters' because they actually floated on water and thereby removed that despair every golfer experiences when a shot plunges into the depths.

In 1921, the R & A, in conjunction with the United States Golf Association, decided to introduce precise specifications for the production of golf balls. The weight of the ball should not be more than 1.62 oz (46 g) and the size not less than 1.62 in (41 mm). This agreement lasted ten years until 1931 when the Americans legalized a larger ball of not less than 1.68 in (43 mm) in

diameter and not heavier than 1.55 oz (44 g). A year later, the weighting was revised upwards to 1.62 oz (46 g) and this is how it stands to this day. The British stuck with the 1.62/1.62 version and the battle began. The British believed that the small ball was more suitable for the tight fairway lies usually found on links courses, while the Americans thought their ball more suited to the lusher grasses in their country. The constant stream of successes by the Americans over the British in all international encounters finally led the British to accept that perhaps the larger ball did encourage improved striking since it had to be 'driven' with a firm action while the smaller ball could be flicked away with a more wristy style.

The larger ball was first used in a professional tournament in Britain in 1960, mainly as a promotional gimmick, but Christy O'Connor completed four rounds at Wentworth in a total of 277 and the die was cast. In 1964, the British PGA made the large ball compulsory for all its events and although this ruling was abandoned the following year, it was reintroduced in 1968 and has remained in force ever since. The PGA regulation did not apply to amateur golf, nor to the Open Championship in which most competitors were playing the small ball. In 1971 the idea of a universal ball of 1.66 in (42.5 mm) was pursued but was dropped mainly because of the expensive

(fig.1)

(fig.3)

(fig.5)

Below and below right
Golf balls being produced at the Penfold factory.

re-tooling that would have been needed to make them.

The 1974 Open Championship marked the watershed of both size balls when the R & A made the large ball compulsory for all competitors. Since then the small ball has been fighting a

Dunlop's explanation of its DDH dimple pattern issued by their Press Office in June 1982. (fig 1) The octahedron shape is the basis of the dimple layout on conventional golf balls. (fig 2) The dodecahedron is a solid figure with twelve identical pentagonal faces and constitutes the basis of the dimple layout on the original Dunlop DDH golf ball and the new Dunlop Marathon DDH. (fig 3) A conventional golf ball showing the 'equators', representing the planes of symmetry through the ball. (fig 4) The unique Dunlop DDH dimple pattern has ten planes of symmetry ('equators'). (fig 5) The Dunlop DDH dimple pattern is based around the twelve pentagonal sides of a dodecahedron. (fig 6) Detail of the DDH dimple layout. This pattern is repeated on each of the twelve faces.

the cover is much more easily damaged.

Initial velocity restrictions have now been standardized to 250 feet per second (76.2 mps) with a two per cent tolerance, and this has stimulated research into the aerodynamic efficiency of golf balls, in other words into their dimple depth and configuration. Golf balls with shallow dimples will fly lower than balls with deeper dimples; golf balls with more dimples on the surface will perform more efficiently than those with fewer dimples. So the battle for golf-ball supremacy goes on with each manufacturer claiming that their ball is the longest- and the highest-flying and the most durable. Is the evolution of the golf ball now complete? Probably not, for as the guttie replaced the featherie only to be replaced itself by the rubber-cored ball, so it appears that man's constant search for perfection of that small, dimpled spheroid will continue. The only certainty is that millions of golfers will still not be sure where it will go when they hit it.

Some of the many balls now on offer to the modern golfer.

rearguard action as the number of its users has rapidly diminished. It is still legal tender among club golfers playing under R & A Rules but with fewer and fewer being sold each year, it is inevitable that it will eventually disappear.

The large ball now reigns supreme and is available in two basic forms: as a one-piece centre with cover, or as a traditional wound centre with cover. Covers are now manufactured from hard-wearing synthetic materials, mostly Surlyn, which are highly resistant to cutting or abrasions. The wound ball is now promoted with a balata cover for the very advanced player or professional since it provides more feel off the clubface and is easier to control around the greens, but

GOLF CLUB DEVELOPMENT

It has always been the nature of the ball currently in use which has dictated the way golf clubs have been designed. In the early days the large boxwood balls used by the Dutch 'kolfers' required large-headed clubs, but with the advent of the smaller and lighter featherie ball clubs were refined to a more delicate shape although they were still cumbersome and unwieldy by modern standards.

The expansion of the golf-club industry seems to have come about when those Scottish Kings who once banned golf in favour of archery practice (see Chapter 1) no longer needed to do so. Wars between the English and the Scots were in decline and the role of the archer increasingly redundant. Where, then, could the unemployed bowyer and fletcher now use their skills? 'Aha,' they said to themselves as they trudged back from somewhere in the vicinity of Hadrian's Wall, 'what is this new-fangled pastime I see my countrymen pursuing? Using clubs to hit a ball about on the links. Could be an opportunity for me.'

Such theories may be fanciful, but one of the reasons for the popularity of golf at that time was because archery was backed by an industry that could readily be adapted to the construction of golf clubs. The skills needed to shape an arrow shaft or forge an arrowhead were very compatible with those needed to balance the shaft of a golf club or forge an iron, while years of experience with bows had taught these craftsmen to judge the flex and torsion of a length of wood.

The connection between archery and golf does not end with the equipment that each requires. The two have many skills in common. Both involve the launching of a projectile at a target many yards away, both are conducted in the open and thus are subject to the vagaries of the weather, and both require a certain amount of co-ordination if a shot is to be successfully launched. Happily for the future of golf, the right craftsmen were already available. Once the featherie ball had become established in the 17th

century, the scene was then set for the development of clubmaking into an art.

The earliest description of golf clubs dates back to 1687 when one Thomas Kincaid wrote his *Thoughts on Golve* and stated that the shaft of the club should be of hazel; it should be both long and supple and the head should be at a very obtuse angle to the shaft. The length of the shaft was 45 in (114 cm) while the head was about 5 in (12.7 cm) long and 2 in (5 cm) wide at the widest point; the depth of the face was about 1 in (2.5 cm). The shaft was joined to the head using a long fine splice known as a scared joint; this was glued in position and finished off with whipping taken from the unravelled strands of ship's rope. The head itself was usually made from blackthorn, apple or beech and the face was concave in shape with the leading edge of the sole being bolstered by the insertion of a strip of ram's horn, held in place by glue and wooden peg inserts.

Nearly all the early clubs were made from wood and designed for specific shots. The play club, or driver, had very little loft and was used when the ball was placed on a turret of sand, the forerunner of today's tee-peg. This club was ineffective on the tight lies which abounded on the links courses, so a club with greater loft was introduced which encouraged the technique of baffing, or bouncing the clubhead into the turf just behind the ball in order to get it airborne. This type of club gave rise to the name 'spoon' to describe a fairway wood, since the club helped the player spoon the ball into the air. For shorter approach shots, clubs with even more loft were used until the player was in the vicinity of the hole, whereupon the holing-out club, or putter, was applied.

It was not until the middle of the 19th century that iron clubs began to appear in any quantity. This was because they were more likely to damage a featherie ball which was easily cut, and, as balls were more expensive than clubs – believe it or not – it was more economical to design a new wooden club. Those iron clubs which did exist were only used in extreme situations when it was impossible

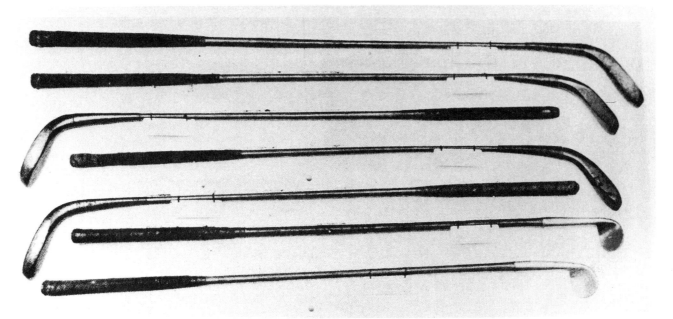

to get a long-headed wooden club to the ball, such as from a cart rut or a mud-filled bunker.

It was a golden age for club-making. By and large the industry consisted of family businesses, some of them operated by men who played the game professionally and augmented their income by manufacturing clubs. Almost all these firms stamped their names on their products and names such as McEwan, Dunn, Patrick, Park, Morris, Forgan and Philp are now woven into the history of the game. Philp, in fact, has become the 'Chippendale' of club-making.

Hugh Philp was born near St Andrews in 1782 and became a clubmaker and repairer in 1812. His business grew and in 1852 he engaged his nephew Robert Forgan as his assistant, by which time another assistant, James Wilson, had left to set up on his own. It has to be assumed that between 1845 and 1852, when he worked for him, Wilson made clubs which bore Philp's name, but it was Forgan who built up the business after Philp's death in 1856 and it continued well into the modern era. The families of Park and Morris are also linked with the history of the Open Championship, since both fathers and sons won it and were able

to cash in on their victories by making clubs which bore their names. Such clubs are now much-prized by collectors and there is a lucrative market among buyers from all parts of the world. At a recent auction, a scared-head long-nosed baffing spoon by Hugh Philp (c. 1840) was sold for £1,600 while a putter from the same maker went for £520.

With the arrival of the guttie ball in 1848, iron club heads suddenly became more popular. One reason for this was that the hard guttie ball inflicted greater damage on wooden clubs than its feather-made predecessor; another was that, although the ball did not cut, it was less responsive and needed a sharper descending blow to make it fly. Woods were still used but they had to be reinforced with leather or vulcanite inserts on the face.

Iron club heads began to dominate the market: there were cleeks or driving irons, lofters, mashies, niblicks, mashie-niblicks, jiggers, sammies and many different types of putter. No longer was it enough for the local blacksmith to produce a few iron clubs as a sideline to his main business; now their manufacture went into full factory production with labour being hired and thousands of irons being forged. The Industrial Revolution

A selection of clubs displayed in the Wood Collection in Manchester.

had arrived in the world of golf, and manufacturers of hand-made clubs went out of business as mass production took over.

All clubs at this stage had shafts made from hickory, which was introduced to Britain from America in 1825. The advantages of this wood over the cruder home-grown hazel shafts were that it possessed a springy, steel-like resilience which meant that much thinner shafts could be fashioned and refined with sandpaper to suit the player. The flexible

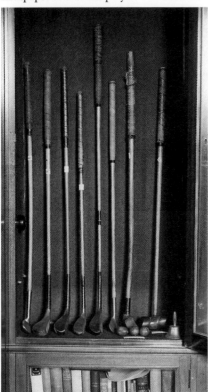

Exhibits in a showcase in the R & A clubhouse.

response of these shafts also enabled players to whip the club through the ball and get more height on the shot. By 1895, over 100,000 hickory shafts per year were being imported from Tennessee to Britain and the finished clubs were beginning to assume the shapes and designs of today's implements.

A major change in the design of woods had taken place in 1885 with the introduction of the 'bulger' driver. The bulger had a short, round head that was about 4 in (10 cm) long, 2–3 in (5–7.6 cm) wide and 1½ in (3.8 cm) deep in the face,

approximately the shape of a modern driver. The important thing about it was that the face was not concave but convex, incorporating the 'bulge and roll' elements that are still found today in drivers. The club was sold on the theory that it cut down on the degree of slice or hook if the ball was struck either on the heel or off the toe.

By the turn of the century, a huge volume of wooden clubs was arriving in Britain from the United States, mass-produced with hickory shafts and persimmon heads. The shafts were now inserted into the heads through a drilled hole and then glued and pinned, a process that was far quicker than the old scared joint. Now that the two major types of wood used in club manufacture were supplied by the United States, the game spread like wild-fire over there, giving that nation a lead in equipment manufacture which it has not really relinquished since.

Persimmon clubheads, hickory shafts and the rubber-cored ball made golf far more enjoyable for the masses and they took to it in droves. Hundreds of membership clubs were formed, as is evident by the number of clubs which have just, or are about to, celebrate their centenaries. No longer were holes measuring 350 yards regarded as two good hits with a play club and a spoon, now they could be reached easily with a driver and a mashie or mashie-niblick. Thus equipment began to exert its influence on golf-course architecture and design. The next stage arrived in 1924 when, seasoned hickory having become more difficult to obtain, the USGA legalized the steel shaft; this move was followed by similar legislation by the R & A in 1929.

The steel shaft did not produce instant power, since the principles of clubhead speed and its application had not changed. What the steel shaft did provide was a marked reduction in torque or twist in the shaft, something that the player using the hickory shaft had to make allowance for during the swing. For this reason the ball could be hit harder using a steel shaft, the player knowing that the torque would be minimal compared with what a hickory shaft would produce.

With one or two exceptions, such as the sand-wedge which was specifically designed to bounce through the sand, the shape of clubs has not changed much over the past 50 years. There have always been fads and gimmicks and there will always be experiments with different materials, such as aluminium and carbon-fibre for shafts, and variations of weight distribution. Even the paradoxically named metal woods, which are currently in vogue, demonstrate that there is very little new under the sun. In 1896, Sir William Mills took out a patent for clubheads made of aluminium which were moderately successful, most particularly the putter called the Braid-Mills which is now a much-sought-after collector's item.

Nowadays, the production centre for the world's clubs has shifted to the Far East and it could be said that any club which is not made in Taiwan is probably made in South Korea. Cheap labour and high production efficiency now dominate the market. Sophisticated advertising and

Right Making the head for a modern wood.

Far right Some colourful examples of contemporary craftsmanship.

Two master craftsmen. Harry Busson (above) in his workshop at Walton Heath, and (above left) Laurie Auchterlonie, for many years the honorary professional to the R & A.

marketing claims, often exaggerated, keep the wheels of commerce turning but the essence of the game is unchanged. It is still the club, the ball, and the player – and the challenge remains eternal.

EQUIPMENT AND TECHNIQUE

Whoever wrote the first instructional book on golf has a great deal to answer for. Translating the written word into a movement that is essentially based on personal feel is something that one player may be able to do but another finds confusing. While the confusion reigns, the golf instruction book will prosper!

That being so, it is still useful to have a look at how equipment has affected the technique of players throughout the development of the game. So back again to Thomas Kincaid, arguably the world's first golf writer, who in his diary *Thoughts on Golve* (1687) expounded the theory of how to play golf as he saw it at that time.

Remember that the clubs then in use were made with a whippy 45 in (114 cm) shaft which entered the clubhead at a very obtuse angle – factors that would have great bearing on the type of swing employed. Kincaid noted that the stance should be closed, with the left foot well forward and the knees slightly bent with the weight favouring the right foot. The ball should be positioned towards the left foot. The body should be bent slightly forward and all the power in the stroke should be generated from the turn of the body. The arms should be held rigid and the grip must be firm. The backswing and forward swing should be performed in one rhythmic motion and the ball should be swept away without the club contacting the turf.

That advice contains a number of points that are still valid today but because of the flat lie of the club the swing would have been very long and rounded and the power would have been accumulated by a big shoulder turn and a gradual acceleration of the club into the ball. Because hazel is a very whippy wood, the shaft would have been extraordinarily thick, thereby necessitating a grip with the shaft held in the palms. The golfer

would have had to 'wait for it' as the ponderous weight of the club moved into the ball; any attempt to whip the club into the ball with the hands would have been disastrous.

The arrival of the hickory shaft and the guttie ball, with the consequent emergence of iron clubs, brought about more changes. Shafts were now shorter and the swings became more upright as players used their hands and arms more in order to get the unresponsive guttie into the air. Golf was very much a low-flying game in the 19th century, ideally suited to the links courses and the turbulent weather of Scotland.

When the rubber-cored Haskell ball emerged at the turn of the century, the situation was completely reversed. The problem now lay in keeping the ball down since it tended to climb up on the clubface at impact. Achieving distance was no longer the prime concern, and swings became shorter and more controlled. The right elbow, which floated well away from the body in swings for the featherie and guttie balls, was now held more tightly to the torso while the shaft, instead of pointing towards mid-off at the top of the swing, was now pointing more towards the target. Hickory enabled shafts to be of thinner construction and the grip was contained more in the fingers, gradually evolving into what is now called the Vardon grip.

This grip was not in fact invented by Harry Vardon, the six-times Open Champion; it had been in existence some twenty years before his arrival on the scene, but there is no question that he popularized it. Vardon was the architect of the modern swing for he demonstrated that brute force was not the key to success. He stood lightly to the ball with a fairly narrow stance and relied on rhythm and timing to sweep the ball away. He showed his contemporaries that golf was a game of control and accuracy and the pin-pointing of his shots became legendary. The old story that he could never play the same course twice in one day because his tee shots in the afternoon would have finished in the divot holes he had made in the morning was, of course, pure fancy –

How to develop the perfect swing. Modern technology is constantly trying to find the answer . . . to sell worldwide to all those millions who aspire to a single-figure handicap.

More aids to perfection.

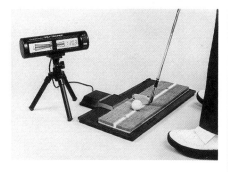

Man-made perfection
achieved via the
ultimate testbed for
balls and equipment.

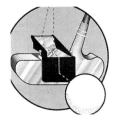

A host of solutions proposed by manufacturers to compensate for the golfer's own inadequacy on the putting surface.

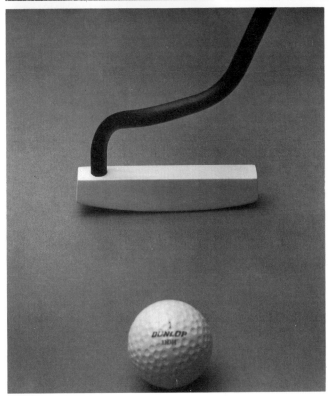

How to produce the perfect golf club.
Below The Petron length and lie gauge and (right) machinery developed by True Temper to test their shafts.

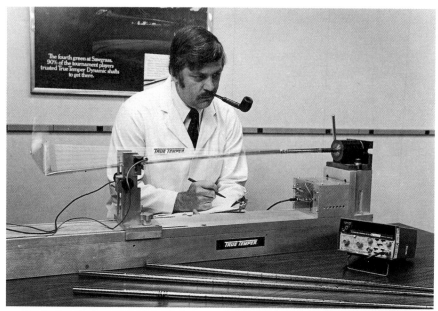

particularly as he himself abhorred the taking of divots!

At the beginning of the 1930s, hickory was on the way out and its last great exponent was Bobby Jones. The prodigy from Atlanta had what was called a 'Carnoustie Swing' since he had been

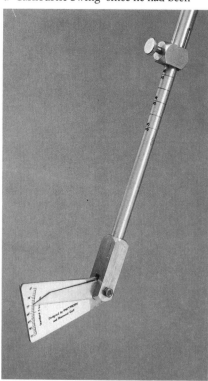

taught by Stewart Maiden, an émigré from that part of Scotland. Jones's swing was lithe and smooth with a full shoulder turn and a marked hip turn. It was also long by modern standards and, again, there was no indication of a hit *at* the ball, it was still clipped away. The torque that existed in hickory shafts meant that timing was the watchword and Jones had it to an exemplary degree. Golf at this time was still being played with the small ball and the timing of the wrist snap into the ball had to be precise.

The legalization of the steel shaft and the adoption of the larger ball in America brought about major changes in technique. The reduction of torque in steel shafts meant that the ball could be driven forward with a more rigid arm action. The Americans also discovered that the larger ball tended to fly higher than its British counterpart and was also more susceptible to any side spin. British players tended to flick the ball away with the hands while the Americans developed the technique of driving through the ball in an effort to keep the ball on the clubface for the maximum time and reduce its tendency to fly high and to cut down on side spin. The superiority of this technique quickly became evident as American players set about their domination of world golf.

GOLF'S GREATEST CHALLENGES

Golf is unique among games in that the arena designated for combat covers such a large area. There are no pitches or courts in golf and thus very few restrictions on where the ball can be hit. It is a game played in conjunction with Nature and it is this harmony (or otherwise) which gives golf its incomparable fascination.

There are thousands of golf courses throughout the world, some still in the early stages of construction, others which have been played over for centuries. All of them provide, or will provide, a degree of pleasure to every player who sets foot on them whether it be for the sheer challenge they present or simply as a place for fresh air and exercise. There are courses set on parkland, on meadowland, on mountains and beside the sea, and some have even been constructed in deserts. Some courses are awash with water hazards, others swarming with bunkers, some will have tree-lined fairways, others with nary a tree in sight, some will be inordinately long, others extremely short. Each will be different from the other so that a golfer could spend a lifetime travelling the world and still find something fresh and stimulating.

Of course, there are also degrees of stimulation and this is where the golfer has to make a judgment as to what constitutes a great course, a good course or an indifferent one. This judgment should not be based on how the golfer fared through the round – a bad score doesn't necessarily mean a bad course – but should be formed objectively. For example, would the course provide equal enjoyment to all golfers, no matter what their standard? Could the golfer, at the end of the round, sit down and have instant recall of every hole? Did the course draw on the full repertoire of his strokes from controlled drives to delicate pitches? Did the holes cause him to think and assess what was required before hitting each shot? Finally, and perhaps most importantly so far as the average golfer is concerned, was it a course where he could happily play for the rest of his days without staleness ever dulling the pleasure?

These are the criteria for a memorable course and the game has been fortunate in having had course architects who have imbued these fundamentals with a creative instinct which elevates their designs above the rest. These courses stand as memorials to their talents and have assumed the mantle of greatness; even so, nearly all the courses which have achieved fame or notoriety owe their present standing to a strip of land hard by the coast near a small Fifeshire fishing town.

St Andrews is the original masterpiece. Some say that God was so preoccupied with the business of Creation that He devised the Old Course as a sort of practice ground for the Real Thing. The truth is rather more ordinary: the Old Course simply emerged and evolved. Its basic design has not changed over the centuries and its problems are still severe despite the modernization of equipment and the improved physical prowess of the current top players.

Some golfers begin by believing that the Old Course is a pushover if they hook the ball around it since most of the trouble, particularly the out-of-bounds, is

on the right. Any golfer who follows this route will find a veritable Pandora's Box of trouble and will quickly reassess his game plan.

The legacy that the Old Course has left to golf is probably best encapsulated in three holes, the 11th, the 14th and 17th. The 11th, or High Hole, is a short hole of 172 yards (157 m) and one

The Old Course, looking out across the historic links.

31

A packed grandstand interrupts the sweep of the Eden estuary behind the 7th and 11th greens.

of the most copied in the game. Played out towards the Eden estuary which lies over the back of the green, the hole is guarded by two deep bunkers, the Strath on the front or right-hand side and the Hill on the left. The pin is often tucked in behind the Strath, and if the golfer is overstrong with his tee shot, a putt of daunting proportions has to be faced down a precipitous slope and the ball can easily finish up in the very bunker that dictated the terms from the tee. It was here that Bobby Jones, playing in his first Open at St Andrews in 1921, took six and then tore up his card, vowing never to return. Fortunately, he did, and triumphed there in 1927. In the 1933 Open, Gene Sarazen finished one stroke out of the play-off between Densmore Shute and Craig Wood having taken three strokes to emerge from the Strath bunker, a cavern so deep that it is alleged that no-one would have known that Sarazen, not the tallest of men, was in there save for the puffs of sand which appeared over the lip.

The 14th, or Long Hole, is 567 yards (518 m) long and strewn with disaster. From the tee, the out-of-bounds wall creeps insidiously into the fairway from the right, automatically pushing the player's aim towards the grasping set of five bunkers on the left, known as the Beardies. If the fairway is found, named the Elysian Fields after the Greek abode of the dead, the decision has to be made whether to carry the enormous Hell bunker with the second or play to the left or right of it. Either route leaves a perilous approach over a steeply sloping bank to the green. In the 1939 Open Bobby Locke came to the 14th standing at five under par and then hooked his tee shot in a strong wind into the Beardies. His attempted recovery was too ambitious and he left the ball in the sand. His fourth shot found Hell and he finished with an eight. The aforementioned Sarazen also took eight there in 1933 following a clash with Hell bunker, and even Peter Thomson's serene progress to the second of his three consecutive Open titles in 1955 was shaken when he tangled with the Beardies to take seven. In the 1984 Open, with the full might of modern technology

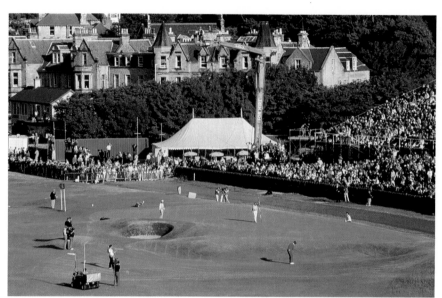

A television gantry hovers, in anticipation of drama, above the 17th green.

at his command, American Bill Rogers, who had won the Open in fine style at Royal St George's three years earlier, contrived to put three tee shots over the wall and walked off with an 11.

And so to the 17th. Ever since David Ayton took 11 here to lose the 1885 Open by two strokes, the Road Hole has been assured of its place in Open tragedy. It is 461 yards (422 m) long and a par four but that figure is irrelevant to even the greatest exponents, most of whom would take a five and walk gladly to the 18th tee. The hole is a marvellous example of the use of angles to confuse and frustrate. From the tee, the presence of the out-of-bounds on the right instinctively draws the aim away to the left. But the further left the tee shot goes, the more invisible becomes the target of the green. And what a target. The front of the green rises alarmingly on to a narrow shelf and, again, the angle of the green in relation to the approach means that any shot slightly overhit will skitter through onto the dreaded road. That really should be enough but Nature has conjured up one more impossible trick in the shape of the Road bunker on the left of the green, a bubbling pot of perdition which gnaws into the putting surface.

In the 1978 Open, Japan's Tsuneyuki 'Tommy' Nakajima wrote his name in the record books. On the front of

the green in two shots, Nakajima putted up the slope only to watch in disbelief as his ball curved gently left and plopped into the Road bunker. The Sands of Nakajima had been excavated four times before he got the ball out, eventually holing in nine.

Because of its position at the end of a round, the Road Hole has also been the scene for many thrilling and memorable moments. The British and Irish victory in the 1971 Walker Cup was clinched at the 17th by David Marsh's superlative second shot to the green which ended the resistance of his opponent, Bill Hyndman of America. In 1978, Jack Nicklaus secured his third Open title by virtue of a magnificent long putt from the front of the green, while six years later, the Road Hole decided the outcome of the enthralling battle between Severiano Ballesteros and Tom Watson. Ballesteros came to the 17th tied with Watson who was playing behind him. The Spaniard had failed to make four in each of his three previous attempts and had·vowed that he would do so or come back on the Monday, presumably for the play-off, and have another go. His drive finished in the left rough, hardly the best place to exert enough control on the ball to stop it on the green. The stroke, with a 6-iron, appeared almost lackadaisical compared with the lashing impact one usually

The disastrous end to Tom Watson's challenge for the 1984 championship.

associates with Ballesteros but its result was no less telling. The ball landed just to the right of the Road bunker and bounced up onto the green, coming to rest 30 feet from the pin. With his four secure, Ballesteros then executed the *coup de grâce* on the final green with a birdie putt just as Watson found himself with his back against the wall on the 17th, having overshot his target massively from the right half of the fairway.

From St Andrews it is but a short journey across the Tay to Carnoustie, another links course which has played a

major role in the outcome of championships. While the Old Course may be regarded as the epitome of strategic design in that it offers the player a number of routes on each hole and leaves it to him to choose which one suits his ability, Carnoustie is ruggedly and brutally penal. From the start, the course demands golf of an impeccable order if a decent score is to be built, and even a sound foundation can be mercilessly ripped out by the severity of the final three holes.

The Open was first staged at Carnoustie in 1931 and last held there in 1975. That first Carnoustie Open resulted in victory for the native-born Tommy Armour who had emigrated to the United States after World War I. Armour won by one stroke from Argentina's Jose Jurado who wrote the first chapter in the book of Carnoustie's finishing holes by taking six on the 17th in the final round. The 17th, 454 yards (415 m) long, is intersected twice by the Barry Burn, requiring the

At Carnoustie the sea comes clearly into view at the 15th.

golfer to carry at least one strip of water with the tee shot. This Jurado did but he then lifted his Latin head on the second and topped the ball into the second strip of the burn. The 18th again has two sections of the burn crossing it with the second part lying just in front of the green. Jurado, unaware of his position in the Championship, played it safely in five only to discover that his earlier six had meant he needed a four to tie.

For the 1975 Open, the 18th was shortened from a par five to a par four of 448 yards (410 m). Tom Watson birdied the hole on the final afternoon with a drive and short iron to ten feet. This put him in a tie with Australia's Jack Newton, and in the play-off the following day Watson produced a 2-iron to the heart of the 18th green to take the title by a single stroke.

Completing this trilogy of terror is the 16th, quite possibly the toughest par three in the world. The hole is 235 yards (215 m) long with two fronting bunkers and a green shaped like an upturned saucer. The tee shot must be long and straight if the ball is not to fall away off the green leaving a chip of infinitely delicate proportions. In his valiant but eventually futile chase of Gary Player in the 1968 Open, Jack Nicklaus struck a full-blooded drive into the teeth of the wind to put the ball 20 feet from the pin, a stroke of staggering quality. Alas, he missed the birdie and Player went on to win by two strokes.

In most people's minds, Carnoustie inspires visions of Ben Hogan and his incomparable victory in the 1953 Open, but it also has equal associations with Henry Cotton who took his second Open title there in 1937 against the full might of the recently victorious American Ryder Cup team. The final round was played in continuous torrential rain and Cotton's round of 71 could be regarded as perhaps his finest. It is indicative that Carnoustie demands nothing less from those who wish to conquer it.

Throughout the history of the Open Championship it is the Scottish courses which have played the dominant role. Prestwick, where the first Open was held in 1860, Royal Troon and Turnberry make an impressive west coast trio. Although Prestwick has not been used for an Open since 1925, holes such as the 3rd, with its huge sleepered Cardinal cross-bunker, the 5th with its blind tee shot over a dune and the 17th with its blind approach over the Alps dunes must have presented a daunting prospect in the days of the guttie ball.

Troon is still on the Open rota and will stage the Championship in 1989. Its most famous hole is the 8th, 126 yards (114 m) long, known universally as the Postage Stamp because of the small green which is heavily guarded by deep bunkers. The hole was also the scene of the second highest score in the Championship's history when, in 1950, a German amateur

Carnoustie's 18th green, protected by the Barry Burn.

Macdonald Smith plays a chip shot to the 13th green during the last Open Championship to be held at Prestwick in 1925.

Sunset over the Postage
Stamp 8th at Troon.

called Hermann Tissies took 15 strokes to hole out after ping-ponging his ball across the green from one bunker to another. One player who did lick the Postage Stamp was Gene Sarazen who holed in one there in the 1973 Open. Troon provides a rugged test, particularly over the inward half where the wind invariably quarters over the left shoulder.

The majestic cliff-top setting of Turnberry had been the venue for many tournaments and championships but never the Open. Its scenic qualities could not be ignored, however, and in 1977 the R & A took the Open there for the first time. The result was the lowest 72-hole aggregate in the history of the event but, to be fair, there was little wind that week and the course was bathed in sunshine. Four years earlier, Turnberry had wrought havoc among the competitors in the John Player Classic when gale-force winds swept across the course, and it was to be no pushover when the Open returned there in 1986 and no-one finished under the stiff par of 280 after 72 holes. Visually the most compelling hole, the 9th begins from a tee built on a rocky promontory next to the cliff edge, and the drive must be struck over a foaming inlet below. The tee itself is a little fraudulent since it is not a work of nature but was built from the torn-up runways that infected the course when it

was used as an airfield during both World Wars. However, no-one would deny that the tee provides the death-or-glory challenge so relished by golfers, even though the carry itself is not enormous.

Water of a less turbulent nature plays its part on Turnberry's 16th, a par four of 415 yards (379 m) with the green perched on a knoll, beneath which trickle the innocuous waters of the Wee Burn. Generations of golfers have watched in anguish as their second shot has landed on the front banking of the green and rolled back into the water. None was more anguished than the members of the 1963 British and Irish Walker Cup team who threw away the chance of victory against the Americans by constantly failing to take enough club on this treacherous hole.

The burn in front of the 16th green at Turnberry.

The 9th tee at Turnberry holds no terrors for Seve Ballesteros during the 1986 Open, watched here by Roger Chapman and his caddy.

To omit Royal Dornoch from any list of great Scottish courses would be an unforgivable oversight. Because of its northerly location and inaccessability it has not staged many championships but it was given its due recognition in 1985 when the British Amateur was held there, resulting in a win for Ulster's Garth McGimpsey. Curving along the shores of Embo Bay at the mouth of the Dornoch Firth, the course is true linksland wandering through banks of whin bushes. Near the turn of the century, Old Tom Morris was commissioned to lay out a further nine holes to the nine which already existed but the land needed little interpretation by man to become a classic course. The chief feature of Dornoch is its raised greens which place a premium on chipping for those players who fail to find them with the approach. This is exemplified by the 14th which is 459 yards (420 m) long and contains no bunkers but needs two outstanding shots for its green to be reached. Those who come up short, and there are many, face the choice of pitching over the slope to the green or running the ball up the bank.

The influence of Dornoch on American course architecture must also be recognized. This influence was spread by Donald Ross, the club's professional for four years, who emigrated to America at the turn of the century and designed over 500 courses in that country. His most eloquent monument, the No. 2 course at Pinehurst, North Carolina, features the basic character of Dornoch's raised greens which create such delicate chipping situations. In addition, Ross was also responsible for Seminole in Florida, a course much respected by Ben Hogan, Oak Hill in New York, Inverness in Toledo, Ohio, and Scioto in Columbus, Ohio, the course where Jack Nicklaus grew up.

The finest of the Scottish links courses has been saved until last. Muirfield, home of the Honourable Company of Edinburgh Golfers, stands supreme as the fairest test of all the seaside courses. Lying on the southern shores of the Forth, the course is bounded by a grey wall on three sides with the northern side protected by buckthorn-covered dunes. These boundaries create the privacy for which Muirfield is famous, a privacy which is jealously guarded by the membership. The course is open and honest, with only one blind tee shot, so the player can see exactly what has to be done on each hole. It is a course which places a premium on accurate driving: any visits to the thick, tangly rough mean the loss of at least a stroke.

There are 18 superb holes waiting

Patterns of green at Muirfield.

The elevated and well protected green at Muirfield's short 13th.

The enormous island bunker beside the 18th green at Muirfield.

to draw upon every stroke in the golfer's repertoire and perhaps it is invidious to select any of them as having particular merit over the others. Tom Watson, however, had no difficulty in making a choice following his victory in the 1980 Open. His selection was the 13th, 153 yards (140 m) long and played to a tightly-bunkered raised green set amid the dunes – a hole that Watson said he would like to package up and ship back to America. It was on the 13th in the 1972 Open that Tony Jacklin took six during the third round but still finished with a 67. The climax to that Championship came at the 17th on the final day when Lee Trevino perpetrated his outrageous chip-in to deliver the final body blow to Jacklin's hopes. The 17th is a par five of 542 yards (495 m) which dog-legs gently to the left. At the corner of the curve, a seething nest of bunkers waits to catch the drive which has attempted to bite off too much from the corner. Further up the fairway lies a group of cavernous cross-bunkers to catch the timid second shot, while the green is protected by two fronting bunkers and a large mound on the right.

Above all, Muirfield is a great watching course with its inner and outer runs of nine holes, which means that no hole is more than a few minutes walk from the clubhouse. This design ensures that the wind is hardly ever in the same direction on consecutive holes and the golfer has to remain aware of the changing problems it presents. The greatness of Muirfield is apparent to all who appreciate that bold, accurate golf should receive its just reward.

The North West coastline of England provides a positive plethora of championship links from a cluster of

courses in Southport, north to Royal
Lytham & St Annes in Blackpool and
south to Hoylake on the Wirral Peninsula.
Of them all, the Royal Liverpool Club at
Hoylake has the longest pedigree; indeed,
after Westward Ho! in Devon it is the
second oldest seaside course in the
country. Hoylake's traditions are rooted
firmly in amateur golf, and the club was
responsible for starting the Amateur
Championship in 1885 and also staged the
first international of all, the England
versus Scotland encounter of 1902. It also
inaugurated the first international match
between Britain and America in 1921, the
forerunner of the Walker Cup. Its most
famous son is John Ball, eight times
winner of the Amateur Championship
and, in 1890, the first amateur and the
first Englishman to win the Open. He was
closely followed by Harold Hilton,
another son of Hoylake, who won the
Amateur four times, the US Amateur once
and the Open Championship twice, the
first time at Muirfield in 1892 when the
Championship changed from 36 to 72
holes.

The 11th at Hoylake
during the 1981 European
Open.

John Ball playing from a
bunker in front of the 4th
green at Hoylake.

Hoylake is unique among
championship courses in that it is possible
to be out-of-bounds within the confines of
the course. The large practice ground to
the right of the 1st hole is bounded by a
turf wall, or 'cop', and over the wall is out
of play. This features comes into the
reckoning for both the drive and second
shot to the 1st and then returns again to
haunt the golfer on the 15th and 16th.
The last five holes represent one of the
most gruelling finishes to be found
anywhere, totalling 2,318 yards (2,120 m)
in length and with out-of-bounds
threatening on three of them. The second
shot to the 17th – 418 yards (382 m) – can

Above Suburban surroundings for the 9th at Lytham.

Above right Arnold Palmer reads the plaque on the 17th at Lytham which commemorates Bobby Jones's historic shot in 1926.

be most taxing and a shot struck with the merest trace of slice can slide away on the wind to roll underneath the boundary fence to the right of the green. Great champions abound at Hoylake from Ball and Hilton to Bobby Jones, who won the second leg of his Grand Slam there in 1930 despite taking seven at the 8th in the final round, to Peter Thomson and Roberto de Vicenzo who won the last Open to be played at Hoylake, in 1967.

Royal Lytham & St Annes does not appear to be a seaside course since the sea cannot be seen from any hole and the course is bounded by the red-brick of well-to-do suburbia. It is an honest test with few weaknesses and possesses a finish at which many potential champions have lost their way. A score must be built over the first nine holes at Lytham in order to leave some strokes in reserve for the long haul home. Most of Lytham's great moments have thus been condensed into the final three holes and, of these, Bobby Jones's second shot from the scrubland to the left of the 17th fairway is certainly the most famous. Locked in deadly combat with his playing companion Al Watrous for the 1926 Open title, Jones hooked into this wilderness while Watrous was down the middle and on the green in two. Jones found his ball lying on sandy wasteland but managed to get enough club to the ball to send it soaring over the trouble onto the green to finish inside Watrous's ball. 'There goes 100,000 bucks,' Watrous is alleged to have said as he saw that stroke, and three putts later he was

right. Lytham holds a special place in the hearts of British golf followers for it was here that Tony Jacklin ended a victory drought for Britain when, after a gap of 18 years, he captured the 1969 Open. The climax to that unforgettable day came at the final hole when Jacklin lay two strokes ahead of his nearest challenger, Bob Charles, the New Zealander who had also won the Open at Lytham six years earlier. The 18th provides the most demanding final tee shot of any British links. The hole is only 386 yards (353 m) long but running into the fairway from the left is a group of seven bunkers lined up to catch any stroke with a hint of pull about it, while on the right lies a formidable spinney of bushes. Threading the eye of this particular needle was beyond the capabilities of Eric Brown, Christy O'Connor and Argentina's Leopoldo Ruiz in the 1958 Open: they all bunkered their tee shots when a straight drive may have given them glory, and Jack Nicklaus's hopes were destroyed in similar fashion in 1963.

Jacklin, however, rose to the occasion magnificently and with a smooth, unhurried swing rifled the ball unerringly down the fairway to make the Championship his. Severiano Ballesteros's victory in the 1979 Open was notable for the lack of time he spent on the fairway, highlighted by his famous 'parking lot' drive on the 16th in the final round. This stroke into the right hand rough was deliberate for it meant that Ballesteros was then pitching into the wind to find the

The solitude of Royal Birkdale.
Left The 2nd green.
Below The view from the tee at the 12th.

Far left Archie Compston battles with the willow-scrub at Birkdale in 1930.

green, rather than with the wind if he had been in the fairway. The tactical sense of this approach was confirmed when he birdied the hole to virtually sew up the title and maintain Lytham's curious record of never to date conceding an Open to an American professional.

Of that cluster of courses in the Southport area, Royal Birkdale is the one which stands supreme. It is not a seaside course of traditional design for although the dunes reach stunning height, the fairways do not go over them but run between in a series of green ribbons. This creates a feeling of solitude rarely found on such an exposed landscape, a solitude that can be rudely interrupted by the anguished cries of golfers trying to extract their ball from the cloying willow-scrub rough. Birkdale is no place for wayward drivers, straightness is the watchword as is

Banks of gorse at Ganton.

The tree-lined fairway of
the 5th at Sunningdale.

shown by the fact that Peter Thomson, a master of accurate wooden club play, won two of his five Open titles there in 1954 and 1965. That 1954 Open was Birkdale's first but it had also staged the 1946 Amateur, won by James Bruen, he of the legendary looping swing, and since World War II championships and international matches have flocked to its gates.

The climax to Tony Jacklin's golden year of 1969 occurred at Birkdale when he and Jack Nicklaus fought out their epic halved match in the Ryder Cup to bring about the first tie between Britain & Ireland and America. Two years later Jacklin was involved in the battle for the Open title, eventually won by Lee Trevino by one stroke from Taiwan's Lu Liang Huan, affectionately known as 'Mr Lu'. Trevino's victory margin would have been greater if he had not drifted off the straight and narrow on the 71st hole by hooking into the huge sand dune which guards the entrance to the 17th fairway, an error which cost him a seven. Tom Watson also visited the same spot on his way to victory in the 1983 Open but he escaped with a five and then sealed his win with a magnificent 2-iron second to the 18th green. Arnold Palmer's first Open title in 1961 is commemorated by a plaque on the 16th from where the great man ripped out a 6-iron shot from the rough onto the green on his way to a win by one stroke from Dai Rees (the hole was the 15th in those days). Johnny Miller completes the list of Open winners at Birkdale (1976), a Championship which first saw the emergence of a young Spaniard named Ballesteros. Clearly, Birkdale is no place for mugs.

By tradition, the Open is always played on seaside courses which owe little or nothing to man's intervention. If we move inland then man's role as a golf-course architect finds its fulfilment in many splendid examples. Ganton in the eastern flank of Yorkshire is a particularly fine test laid out by Harry Vardon, who was professional there, and Tom Dunn with additions by Harry Colt. Set in the Vale of Pickering a few miles from Scarborough, Ganton is a heathland course featuring large, deep bunkers amid

banks of gorse. The 18th, a left-hand dog-leg of nearly 400 yards (366 m), is a testing finishing hole which has often resolved the outcome of the many Amateur Championships and professional tournaments which have been held there.

Vardon also had a hand in another superb inland test, that of Woodhall Spa in Lincolnshire. The present course was reconstructed after World War I by the Hotchkin family which owned the land, and fully utilizes the heather, broom and silver birch topography. What bounty this type of land has yielded to golf. Nowhere has the harvest been more richly reaped than on a stretch of country to the west of London. In this area of pine, birch, heather and firm, sandy subsoil is a multitude of truly outstanding courses. Sunningdale, Wentworth, Walton Heath and The Berkshire are the names which readily spring to mind with Sunningdale being the one course where most golfers would happily spend the rest of their days.

The Old Course at Sunningdale was laid out at the turn of the century by Willie Park Junior, twice Open Champion, who was paid the princely sum of £3,800 for the commission. He created an enchanting work, featuring a number of short par-four holes, the finest of which is the 325 yard (297 m) 11th. This hole is reachable from the tee for the siege-gun driver, but what menace awaits for the stroke which veers off-line. Running along the right-hand edge of the fairway up to the green is a tall stand of pines while a deep bunker and more trees lie in wait for the hook. From the fairway a pitch of exacting requirement is faced, for the green possesses a slight crown in the middle, and the pin is usually placed beyond it.

The Old Course also witnessed what is often quoted as the perfect round of golf when Bobby Jones holed it in 66 strokes in the qualifying for the 1926 Open, which he went on to win. The round contained 33 putts and 33 other shots with every hole completed in three or four. Sunningdale is the sort of course which inspires such perfection.

Wentworth, just down the road from Sunningdale, has gained great exposure through the televising of the World Match-Play Championship held there every autumn. It is a long course, maybe too long for the average player, requiring strong accurate driving and quality iron play. Its most famous hole is the 17th, a curving par five containing only one bunker and dominated by an out-of-bounds running along the entire left-hand side. The drive is quite terrifying as the out-of-bounds creeps in from the left, forcing the ball to be kept to the right. The fairway slopes sharply to the right

The 1st fairway at Wentworth looking back towards the clubhouse.

A testing drive from the 15th tee on the Red course at The Berkshire.

towards a clump of trees. From the fairway, the second shot is played over the brow of a hill which drops down to a flat, unencumbered green which demands great judgment of depth for the pitch. The hole has been, and will continue to be, the graveyard of many hopes. A similar rugged test exists at Walton Heath where the 16th on the Old Course, a long two-shotter to a raised green, stands out as a great hole by anybody's standards while The Berkshire provides golf in tranquil natural surroundings of great beauty over two courses, the Red and the Blue.

Our final English destination has to be the last of the great British links, Royal St George's at Sandwich, Kent. The history of St George's is long and glorious. Founded in 1887, the club in 1894 staged the first Open to be held outside Scotland, which J. H. Taylor won, and the course

quickly established itself as a severe examination of skill. Its holes progress through a desolate expanse of dunes and its fairways dip and rise in switchback fashion to greens that are heavily guarded. Walter Hagen, Henry Cotton and Bobby Locke are numbered among the champions who won there, and after Locke's victory in 1949 – the Championship containing the infamous broken bottle incident which affected Harry Bradshaw's run for the title – the Open did not return there until 1981, having stayed away because of poor road access.

The course has staged the Amateur Championship on many occasions and various professional tournaments. The short 16th witnessed the first televised hole-in-one during the 1967 Dunlop Masters tournament when

Far left The dunes and valleys of Royal St George's.

Left Henry Cotton plays from the edge of the 6th green on his way to victory at Royal St George's in the 1934 Open.

Cavernous bunkers on the 4th at Royal St George's.

Tony Jacklin, on his way to a winning final round of 64, achieved this feat. Following the resurrection of the course as a modern Open venue in 1981, the Championship quickly returned there and in 1985 Sandy Lyle became the first British winner since Jacklin in 1969. Lyle suffered agonies on the final hole, a stiff par four of 442 yards (404 m) with a solitary bunker on the right of the green. In steering clear of this hazard, Lyle's second shot trickled off the green into thick rough below a steep bank. This area is known as 'Duncan's Hollow' after George Duncan, the British professional who needed to get down in two from this spot to catch Hagen in the 1922 Open. He failed in his attempt and Lyle ran him close when his chip up the hill was not quite strong enough and the ball ran back to his feet. He bravely got down in two more, however, to write yet another stirring page in the history of British Championship golf.

IRELAND

Before crossing the Atlantic to America, we must pause to recognize the quality of the great links courses in the land across the Irish Sea. Here lies a wealth of magnificent courses, such an abundance indeed that one is put in mind of the visitor to Ireland who, on seeking guidance from a local, was informed: 'If I were you I wouldn't start from here.'

From Royal County Down and Royal Portrush in the North to Ballybunion and Lahinch in the South, Ireland is one long strip of green fairway providing golf of infinite variety. Royal Portrush stands as the only Irish course to stage the Open Championship, which Max Faulkner won in 1951 in conditions which saw only two players break 70 during the whole event. Set amid tumbling dunes, the main course at Portrush is called Dunluce after the ancestral home of the Lords of Antrim. Its layout is the work of many men, primarily Harry Colt who improved it to modern standards and placed a great premium on driving. Only the first and last holes run straight, the rest curve; it is this aspect, rather than the hazards of bunkers and rough, which make it so challenging. Its most famous hole, some would say the most famous in Ireland, is the 14th, 211 yards (193 m) long and aptly named Calamity Corner, which invariably requires a wooden club shot into the wind to a green set on the top of a hill, below which the ground falls away alarmingly to the right into a chasm of rough and misery.

For sheer breathtaking beauty, few courses are the equal of Royal County Down just outside Newcastle (NI). Here the Mountains of Mourne sweep down to the sea and provide a compelling vista for golfers who may find that these distractions compensate them for the constant problem they have to keep their shots out of the banks of flowering gorse which abound. Purists may baulk at the number of blind shots the course possesses but no golfer could be blind to the stunning scenery of the place.

Links golf of an honest, straightforward nature is to be found at Portmarnock on a fine strip of coastland on the northern side of Dublin Bay. Portmarnock's challenge lies in the wind. The holes are laid out on inner and outer runs, and the direction of the wind is constantly varied. Many championships and tournaments have been held at Portmarnock; it is a regular venue for the Irish Open, and provided a fitting setting for one of Christy O'Connor's most memorable victories, in the 1959 Dunlop Masters, when he overhauled his countryman, amateur Joe Carr, with a final round of 66. O'Connor sealed his victory with a superb 4-wood second shot to the 466 yard (426 m) 17th which finished eight feet away for the decisive birdie.

A view of Dublin Bay from the 15th at Portmarnock.

The 4th at Lahinch.

The 13th at Portrush.

Any golfing pilgrimage to Ireland must be made with the ultimate destination in mind, that of Ballybunion at the mouth of the River Shannon in Co. Kerry. En route, the pilgrim may pause at Killarney, whose 18th hole along the shores of Lough Leane prompted Henry Longhurst to comment: 'What a lovely place to die,' or at Ireland's most westerly links, Waterville, or travel north up the coast into Co. Clare where Lahinch is enshrined as the St Andrews of Ireland. These, however, act as appetizers for the links which are universally regarded as the finest in the world, moving Tom Watson to say that Ballybunion is a course where golf architects should live and play before building golf courses. Swooping down among the sandhills with the Atlantic rollers surging in beneath, Ballybunion is quite simply majestic. The club is doubly fortunate in that it now has another course, the New, which is equally splendid, laid out by Robert Trent Jones, the indefatigable American course architect, upon whose creations the sun is said never to set.

Discovering the charm of Irish golf is an experience to be savoured, preferably in a leisurely fashion. The local hospitality is notorious for its generosity but nowhere does the character of Irish golf express itself more eloquently than in this quote by Christy O'Connor of Ballybunion: 'The man who breaks 70 here is playing better than he is able.'

THE UNITED STATES OF AMERICA

Without doubt the greatest influence on American golf course architecture is to be found at the Augusta National Golf Club in Georgia, home of the annual Masters tournament.

Augusta is the shrine of American golf, the place where the faithful come to worship the legend of Bobby Jones, the only man to have won the Open and Amateur titles of both Britain and America in a single year (1930). Following that tumultuous year, Jones retired from competitive golf although aged only 28, but retained the desire to found a private club on a course

The immaculate beauty of the 13th at Augusta.

which he himself would design.

Luckily for golf he found the perfect site – 365 acres (148 ha) of rolling land in the small winter resort of Augusta. The land had been developed as a nursery by a Belgian baron and abounded with azaleas, dogwoods, magnolias and redbuds and the setting was completed by a pre-Civil War mansion overlooking it. Because of his peerless record as a player, any course which Jones put his name to was bound to be influential but in creating his dream course he showed a wisdom beyond his years by combining his knowledge of shot-making requirements with the architectural genius of Alister Mackenzie. Mackenzie was a Scottish-born doctor who had emigrated to America and given up medicine in order to concentrate on golf. He had already shown his flair for design in creating Cypress Point in California and thus had the right credentials for building courses in areas of great natural beauty.

At first sight, Augusta National does not look difficult. Its fairways are generously wide, there is hardly any rough and very few bunkers. The stately Georgian pines separate the holes to create a cathedral-like atmosphere of peace and the flowering shrubs provided a colourful framework which lead the golfer to believe that this truly is paradise on earth. It is only when the course is played that the greatness of its challenge becomes apparent.

Jones wanted a course that would provide equal enjoyment to both professionals and amateurs. If a player is content to go round in one over par on every hole, then the course will not tax that requirement. If, however, a player is looking for pars and birdies then Augusta will stretch his shot-making abilities to the limit. It is a course where planning must start on the tee of each hole, for the placement of the drive will dictate the approach to the green and the position of the flag will dictate on which part of the green the ball should finish. It could be said that it is the greens which set the entire strategy of the course. Huge, slick and undulating, Augusta's greens show the influence of St Andrews on Jones

whose respect for the traditions of the game is captured in their topography.

The course was completed in 1933 and the following year Jones invited his friends, amateur and professional, for his first tournament get-together. The Press also turned up and before the event, won by Horton Smith, was over they had

Horton Smith, winner of the first Masters in 1934.

given it the tag 'The Masters'. A year later came the shot that was heard round the world, setting the pattern for a host of spectacular strokes at The Masters.

The closing stages of the 1935 Masters found Gene Sarazen standing in the middle of the 15th fairway needing three birdies to catch Craig Wood who had already finished. Sarazen faced a shot of some 220 yards carry over the lake in front of the green and since he was in a do-or-die situation, he elected to go for it with a 4-wood. The ball flew unerringly over the water, landed on the green and ran straight into the hole for an albatross. With that one stroke, Sarazen had tied with Wood and when he won the play-off the next day, the Augusta legend had its first foundation stone.

The margin between success and failure has always been extremely fine at Augusta simply because the course constantly tempts the player to bite off a little more than can safely be chewed. Nowhere is this more evident than on the last nine holes, five of which contain water thereby making them the Venice of championship golf. Three of the water holes are in succession and, because of their placing in the round and the

creek and eventually walked off with a 13.

The 13th is an absolutely gorgeous hole of 485 yards (443 m), dog-legging gently to the left. The creek weaves its insidious path along the left side of the fairway before crossing directly in front of an enormous green which slopes down towards the water. Every

psychological pressures they exert, the 11th, 12th and 13th have been dubbed Amen Corner, presumably because if a player gets through them without mishap he gives a prayer of thanks. Of these the 12th, at 155 yards (142 m) the shortest hole on the course, is, in the words of Jack Nicklaus, 'the most psychologically demanding hole in championship golf'. Fronted by Rae's Creek, the green is less than 30 feet in depth with two sloping bunkers at the back and another bunker in the centre-front. Set in a pocket of tall trees, the hole is subject to capricious wind changes which can swirl the ball into the water or into the back bunkers. The 12th has been aced (holed-in-one), but in the pressured atmosphere of the Masters it is more famous for its victimization of players. Most notable of these is Tom Weiskopf who, during the first round of the 1980 Masters, put five balls into the

stroke on this hole must be carefully pondered. If the drive is long and drawn round the corner of the dog-leg then the green can be reached with a long iron; if the drive is out to the right then the decision has to be made whether to go for the carry over the creek or lay up and hope to get down in a pitch and a putt. Many a Masters challenger has seen his hopes plunge into the water through making an incorrect decision when faced with this dilemma. In the 1985 Masters, Curtis Strange looked set to perpetrate the greatest recovery in the history of the event when he opened with an 80 and then followed that with rounds of 65 and 68. Leading in the final round, he put his second to the 13th in the creek and repeated the error on the 15th for a couple of sixes which allowed Bernhard Langer to come through and win. Back in 1937, Ralph Guldahl was leading Byron Nelson

Curtis Strange in trouble at the Creek on the 13th during the final round of the 1985 Masters.

by two strokes but splashed his way through the 12th and 13th in five and six while Nelson played them in two and three to overhaul him for victory. In 1978 Tsuneyuki Nakajima made it a very unlucky 13th for himself when he completed the hole in 13 strokes, five of which were penalty strokes, two being incurred when he tried to play the ball out of the creek and the ball bounced off the bank and hit him.

Thus the legend of Augusta has been built. In the 50-plus years of Masters history, the course has inspired and rewarded the brave, regularly served up the unexpected and treated the world to some of the most spectacular moments in the game. From Sarazen's albatross in 1935 to Jack Nicklaus's unprecedented

sixth green jacket in 1986, from Sam Snead and Ben Hogan to Gary Player and Arnold Palmer, from Tom Watson to Severiano Ballesteros, the list of winners at Augusta includes the greatest names of the era. The present course record stands at 63, set by Nick Price in 1986, but that particularly low score does not detract from Augusta's challenge, it enhances it, for it shows that the man who thinks his way round the course will have fulfilled all the requirements of Bobby Jones's grand design.

While the United States contains a vast number of courses on a variety of landscapes, the country does not possess any traditional linksland as is found in Britain. But, for golf by the sea America is amply compensated by two magnificent

The crashing breakers of the Pacific behind the 7th (above) and 8th (above right) greens at Pebble Beach.

courses on the Monterey Peninsula on the coast of California: Pebble Beach and Cypress Point. They are also enshrined in American golfing folk lore as courses where that harmony between Nature and Man is pitched in exactly the right key.

Faced with such a compelling vista of cliff-top land with the Pacific rolling in beneath, the architects of both courses could have easily gone overboard in their designs. Instead, they showed admirable restraint and stuck to the principle that the best courses are built into the land that is available, and the less Nature is tampered with the better. Pebble Beach has seven holes running along the edge of the cliffs and each of them provides at least one death-or-glory flirtation with the foaming ocean. The

first glimpse of sea occurs at the 4th but it is at the short 7th that the golfer first finds the senses stirred. This short hole of 120 yards (110 m) is played directly towards the crashing breakers with the green entirely surrounded by bunkers and angled on line with the tee so that the target is only eight yards wide. On a still day it is no more than a wedge but with the wind whipping in, a punched medium iron may well be necessary to keep the ball on line. The 8th, 9th and 10th are a trio of gruelling par fours where drives and second shots are fully exposed to the elements of wind and water. The merest hint of a slice can mean either a visit to the beach or a rinse in the world's largest bath. From the 10th the course turns inland and does not return to the cliffs until the 17th and 18th, and it is here that the outcome of many tournaments and championships has been resolved. In the two US Opens staged at Pebble Beach in 1972 and 1982, the 17th was the scene of the decisive strokes. This 218 yard (199 m) par three is played directly towards the sea with the cliffs falling away on the left. The green is long from side to side but narrow from back to front and protected by a large fronting bunker. In 1972, Jack Nicklaus assured his third US Open title when he struck a 1-iron witheringly through the wind almost into the hole. Nicklaus was also involved in the finish of the 1982 Open when he set a target that only Tom Watson could beat. Watson needed two pars to tie but his hopes looked slim when his tee shot to the 17th landed in thick rough to the left of the green. With the pin set on the left side of the green, he had hardly any room to manoeuvre the ball close, but with one of the most memorable strokes in recent times he lobbed the ball gently onto the green and danced in delight as it trickled into the hole. Disaster could still have overtaken Watson on the 18th as the full length of its 540 yards (494 m) is flanked on the left by the sea. Many professionals have seen their hopes dashed on the rocks by going flat out for the green in two shots but Watson played it cannily to be on the green in three, and his birdie putt was merely icing on the cake.

The remarkable thing about Pebble Beach is that it was laid out by two amateur architects, Jack Neville and Douglas Grant, neither of whom did much work elsewhere yet their instinct for the land cannot be faulted. At Cypress Point, however, just a mile away from Pebble Beach, pure genius has been at work. Designed by Alister Mackenzie of Augusta National and Royal Melbourne fame, Cypress Point is regarded by many people as the loveliest golf course in the world. It is only 6,500 yards (5944 m) long and there are just three holes which run along the cliff-tops while the remainder wend their way through sandy dunes and woodland. No major championships have been held there but it is the venue for the annual Bing Crosby

National Pro-Am, now called the AT & T, and every player in the field is aware that the first 15 holes are merely a prelude for the symphony of design that is the 16th.

This hole is preceded by the exquisite minor movement of the short 15th, only 139 yards (127 m) long across the rocky inlet, and then the golfer is faced with what is certainly the most photographed hole in golf. Measuring 233 yards (213 m), the 16th is played across the ocean to a green where the presence of a group of bunkers could be regarded as relief when compared to the perdition that awaits in the rocks and ice-plant below. No worthy golfer could resist the temptation to make at least one attempt to carry the ball all the way to the green, although there is an area of fairway short and to the left for the less brave, or perhaps one should say the less foolhardy. The record highest score for the hole is 19, set in 1959 by a professional named Hans Merrell who clambered down the cliffs to his ball and spent some considerable time among the ice-plant before finally emerging. Appropriately, Bing Crosby himself stands as only one of two golfers, Jerry Pate being the other, to have holed-in-one at the 16th.

Further north on the West Coast lies a course of an entirely different nature. This is the Lakeside course of the Olympic Club Country Club in San Francisco, a cumbersome title that is usually shortened to plain Olympic. Here is golf of a far more penal type, as is generally true of

The spectacular 16th at Cypress Point.

courses built before 1930, an era when architects followed the creed that golf should temper the spirit with excessive hardship. Olympic was constructed in 1922 on sloping land to the west of the city and when the holes were laid out the club then planted hundreds of pine, eucalyptus and cypress trees. Some 25 years later the trees had reached full maturity and created an arboreal nightmare in which golfers were constantly playing through a funnel of trees whose branches appeared to be reaching out to grab the ball. Add to this a number of dog-leg holes where the land slopes in the opposite direction to the flow of the dog-leg and it can be understood why Olympic is a fearsome test, even for the mighty.

Of the three US Opens staged at Olympic, in 1955, 1966 and 1987, the first two provided major upsets. In 1955, Ben Hogan was safely in the clubhouse on the brink of an unprecedented fifth US Open title. Out on the course, only one man could catch him, an obscure professional from Iowa called Jack Fleck. Fleck eventually came to the 338 yard (309 m) 18th needing a birdie three to tie and stunned the golfing world by holing a putt of seven feet to achieve it. In the play-off, Fleck stood one stroke ahead on the 18th tee and Hogan, in attempting to combat the left-to-right camber of the fairway, hooked violently into the left-hand rough from where he needed three strokes to recover; and that was that.

Eleven years later, Arnold Palmer had taken the championship by the scruff of the neck and with nine holes to play was seven strokes clear of his closest challenger, Billy Casper, with whom he was playing. With four holes left to play, Casper still trailed by five shots but by virtue of some brilliant play, coupled with errors from Palmer, had drawn level by the 18th and that is how it remained. Palmer's crisis occurred on the monster 604 yard (552 m) 16th when he strove for distance from the tee and hooked into the rough, finally taking six to Casper's immaculate birdie four. The play-off saw Casper again come from behind to win and demonstrate that Olympic is a course where any attacking instincts of the kind upon which Palmer built his career, must be suppressed.

While Olympic uses trees to intimidate the golfer, across the country in Pennsylvania stands the Grand Vizier of penal design. Split in two by the Pennsylvania Turnpike on the outskirts of Pittsburgh, Oakmont Country Club has the reputation of being the toughest golf course in America. It is a reputation founded on severe bunkering (more than 200 of them) and greens whose swiftness has passed into legend. The course was laid out by steel magnate Henry Fownes in 1904 and his dream of creating a murderous course has been substantiated by a series of high winning scores in the six US Opens that have been held there. The lowest 72-hole aggregate for the US Open at Oakmont is the five-under-par 279 set by Johnny Miller in 1973 which contained a final round of 63, a record round still only matched by Jack Nicklaus and Tom Weiskopf in the 1980 US Open at Baltusrol. Miller's round was certainly helped by the fact that during the previous night heavy rain was accompanied by someone inadvertently leaving the sprinkler system running which turned the greens into dartboards and greatly reduced their terrors.

Prior to Miller's astonishing surge, Bobby Jones, Ben Hogan and Jack Nicklaus had all added to Oakmont's history: Jones through his victory in the 1925 US Amateur when he was never

Arnold Palmer plays out of the famous Church Pews at Oakmont.

taken beyond the 14th in all his matches; Hogan for his awesome last-round mastery of the final four holes which he played in a total of 13 strokes on his way to a five-stroke victory in the 1953 US Open, and Nicklaus for breaking through for his first professional victory in the 1962 US Open after a play-off with Arnold Palmer. From its furrowed bunkers, which used to be raked two inches deep and two inches apart using a special rake, to its lightning fast greens, Oakmont is a course which simply does not tolerate inadequacy in any department.

Cast in a different, rougher mould is Pine Valley, quite possibly the most terrifying course in the golfing universe. The brainchild of George Crump, a Philadelphia hotelier, Pine Valley, on the New Jersey side of that city, took seven years to complete and was opened in 1919. The trees which separate each hole are the least of the golfer's problems for the entire course is laid out on one huge 184 acre (74 ha) bunker with tees, fairways and greens forming havens of refuge amid the sandy wasteland. The psychological pressures of having to hit from one green island to another with absolutely no room for error is too much for most players and there is a standing bet that nobody will break 80 at the first attempt.

Such a bet was irresistible to Arnold Palmer back in 1954 when he was US Amateur champion and desperate for some money prior to his elopement and marriage. He collected all the bets he could find, knowing he couldn't afford to pay them if he lost, and went round in 68. Few golfers are as gifted as Palmer, however, and for many 68 would be a reasonable score for the first nine holes. Pine Valley has never staged the US Open, its layout would not accommodate the crowds, but it has been the venue of two Walker Cup matches, in 1936 and 1985. The most famous story concerning the terrors of Pine Valley, and the mental strain it creates, involves one Woody Platt, a gifted Philadelphia amateur. Platt set off on a round as follows: three (birdie), two (eagle), one (ace), three (birdie). Thus he had played the first four holes in six under par. These first four holes make a full circle back to the clubhouse and Platt decided to retire inside for a restorative glass of something to brace himself for

A sea of sand surrounds the 17th green at Pine Valley.

what lay ahead. Possibly he over-celebrated his hole-in-one for he never emerged to complete the round.

The West Course at Merion on the other side of Philadelphia from Pine Valley is not blessed with any of the naturally rugged terrain of its neighbour. Indeed, Merion's 18 holes are squeezed into a compressed 110 acres (45 ha), barely enough to accommodate some of the more modern courses' parking lots. Yet, for subtlety of design which rewards accurate, attacking golf, it has few equals. The essence of Merion is contained in its greens which are extremely fast, and its greenside bunkering which makes the player think carefully each time about the best line of approach to the target. Merion is only just over 6,500 yards (5,944 m) long and possesses 120 bunkers but each one has been placed in precisely the right position by the architect, Hugh Wilson, who completed his work in 1912.

Great moments at Merion read like a potted history of American golf and it is appropriate that its most famous hole, the 11th, was the scene of the final act in Bobby Jones's Grand Slam year of 1930 when he won the US Amateur by closing

out his opponent in the final by 8 & 7. The 11th, known as the Baffling Brook hole, entirely captures the spirit of Merion. Only 370 yards (338 m) long, it dog-legs gently to the left and the brook, after intersecting the fairway, runs past the right edge of the green which is also protected by a left-hand bunker. For the accomplished player, the hole is no more than a drive and a short iron, but the approach is most exacting as it has to flirt with that ribbon of water. The 18th at Merion is built on a more heroic scale: it is 458 yards (419 m) long, and the drive is played through a funnel of trees to a fairway which runs downhill in the landing area. It was here in the 1950 US Open that Ben Hogan, still hardly recovered from a horrific road accident a year earlier, began his comeback by striking a magnificent 2-iron second shot into the heart of the green to tie for the title. In 1971, Jack Nicklaus repeated that stroke with a 4-iron to tie with Lee Trevino for the US Open. Ten years later in the US Open, Merion was the site of what is generally regarded as the most perfect final round ever played in a major championship, the 67 from Australia's

Treacherous broom grass waiting for the wayward approach shot alongside the 18th green at Merion.

Ancient and modern.
Left A view of the course
at Shinnecock Hills from
above the 18th green.
Below The incredible
17th green at the TPC
course in Florida.

Pete Dye, architect of
some of the most testing
courses to have been built
in recent years.

David Graham who plotted his way to
victory by not missing a fairway or a
green in regulation figures over the entire
18 holes.

From the white-faced bunkers of
Merion in the East to the white-tipped
breakers of the Pacific, America offers
such a variety of courses that it would take
several books to cover them all. Therefore,
apologies must be made for such notable
omissions from this chapter as Baltusrol,
The Country Club, The National,
Winged Foot, Pinehurst, Medinah and
the Hills of Shinnecock, Southern,
Oakland and Oak Hill. They, and many
other superb examples of the architect's
craft, would take a lifetime to examine.

Unlike the great links courses of
Britain and Ireland, which evolved
naturally, golf course architecture in
America is largely a triumph of man's
perception coupled with the mechanical
grab. Such machinery can be used to
dramatic effect, viz. the island 17th green
at the Tournament Players' Club in
Florida or at the new PGA West course in
Palm Springs, both products of Pete Dye,
probably the most creative of modern
designers and certainly the most
controversial.

The challenge to create a lasting
materpiece is one which has fuelled the
desires of architects for nearly a century. In
appreciating the challenge, millions of
golfers have discovered that golf is
indisputably the best game ever invented.

THE MAJORS AND THE
WORLD MATCH-PLAY

As befits the orderly structure of the game, golf's glittering prizes are confined to just four championships: The Open, the US Masters, the US Open and the US PGA. These four are the major championships in professional golf and although the British and US Amateur championships are also referred to as major championships, this is really a throwback to the days when amateurs were also winning Open titles.

There is no question that the Open is the most prestigious of the major championships. Not only is it the oldest, it has also developed into the true world championship of golf with a field of genuine international spread. Traditionally staged on a British seaside links, the Open stands as an enduring connection with the past and among its winners are numbered the greatest names in the game.

The US Masters is the youngest of the big four, first contested in 1934, but because the event was created by Bobby Jones on the course which he himself designed, its elevation to Major status was quickly achieved. The Masters is the only major championship which is played on the same course each year and the glories of Augusta National in the spring always herald the start of a new season. The Masters' one weakness is that the field is not truly representative of world golf in that most of the players receive their invitation to play because they have won an American Tour event or one of the other three major championships. Other invitations are made, and there is always a strong amateur element, but the entry is still American-dominated.

The same could be said of the US Open which began in 1894, but this is mainly due to the geographical problems of overseas players committing themselves to extended periods in America. The US Open is held at different venues each year and in recent years has been the subject of much criticism by the players who believe that the courses have been made too severe in preparation for the championship. Make no mistake, though, the winners of the US Open are generally from the upper stratum of the game and have added lustre to the history of golf.

The last of the four, the US PGA Championship, is something of a hybrid. It began as a match-play event and if it had stayed in that format it would undoubtedly enjoy greater standing than it does today. The demands of television, however, resulted in it changing to stroke-play in 1958 and from then it took on the guise of just another American Tour event. Steps have been taken to raise its status by staging the event on courses which host US Opens and this has helped restore its position.

These four championships represent the modern Grand Slam, a title that was created when Bobby Jones won the Open and Amateur titles of both Britain and America in 1930. Nowadays, no amateur could contemplate repeating Jones's feat so the challenge of winning all four major professional titles in a single year has become the Holy Grail. No player has yet achieved that unlikely quadrilateral, indeed, there are only four players who have won all four titles in their careers – Gene Sarazen, Ben Hogan, Gary Player and Jack Nicklaus. Hogan won three major titles in 1953 – the Masters, US Open and Open – but having triumphed at Carnoustie he could not get back in time to compete in the US PGA, boat rather than jet being the mode of transport. Jack Nicklaus has striven mightily throughout his career to accomplish the feat but the best he has done is two Majors in one year, although he has done this five times and is the only man to have won all four championships more than once in his career. In 1986 Greg Norman became the first player to lead going into the final round of all four, but he ended up by winning just the Open and it may well be that this particular milestone will never be passed.

As the game has exploded over the past twenty years, many pretenders have sought to become a fifth Major. Most of them have tried to achieve this status by providing huge prize funds but this somewhat vulgar approach has resulted in total rejection. Tradition cannot be bought and instant classics can dissolve as quickly as they appeared. Continuity and quality are other essential ingredients, and in this respect the World Match-Play Championship, while not laying claim to being a Major, can certainly be regarded as the captain of all the other tournaments which aspire to such heights. Started in 1964, the World Match-Play Championship was originally conceived to bring together the eight best players in the world during the year and pit them against each other in man-to-man combat. This concept has now been expanded to include 16 players, not all of whom in any given year are from the very top echelon but the event still remains the only genuine match-play championship in the world. It is held every autumn over the West Course at Wentworth and its list of winners reads like a Debrett of the modern era. It has produced some of the most stirring moments in the game and its chief asset is that it keeps alive a form of golf that is virtually extinct at professional level.

THE OPEN

17 October 1860. This date is enshrined in golfing history for on that day, eight professionals gathered on the links of Prestwick to do battle for the first Open Championship. Since there was no amateur involvement, the title 'Open' was incorrect but the main aim of the event at that time was to find a successor to Allan Robertson of St Andrews who, until his death the previous year, had proved to be virtually unbeatable. Willie Park of Musselburgh covered the 12 holes of the 3,799 yard (3,474 m) course in rounds of 58, 59 and 60 to take the prize, a Moroccan leather Championship belt, by two strokes from Tom Morris Senior.

For the first seven years, Park and Morris took a virtual stranglehold on the belt with Morris winning in 1861, 1862, 1864 and 1867 and Park in 1863 and 1866; the only player to break this domination was Andrew Strath in 1865. By now amateurs were competing regularly but the professionals still held sway and if his competitors had not had enough of one Morris, they were about to become thoroughly acquainted with another. In 1868 Young Tom Morris followed in his father's footsteps and at the age of 17 set a new record of 157 for the 36 holes. This youthful prodigy, who still remains the youngest winner of the Open, then lowered that record in winning the next year, and in 1870 he made it three wins in a row with an aggregate of 149,

Willie Park, winner of the first Open Championship in 1860.

Tom Morris Senior, runner-up in the first Open and winner of the Championship four times in the 1860s.

his first 12-hole round of 47 being one under fours and quite extraordinary considering the equipment at his disposal, including the guttie ball.

The Championship belt, presented by the Earl of Eglington, now became Young Tom's property and because there was no alternative trophy available, the Championship was suspended in 1871. Prestwick then approached the R & A and the Honourable Company of Edinburgh Golfers, and the three clubs agreed to take it in turns to stage the Open. They then purchased the famous silver claret jug as a permanent trophy. The Open returned to Prestwick in 1872 and, once again, Young Tom emerged the winner to make it four wins in a row, a record which has never been equalled. St Andrews hosted the event in 1873 for the first time and the winner was Tom Kidd with Young Tom finishing joint third; the following year he was second at Musselburgh to Mungo Park. Tragedy then struck as Young Tom's wife died in childbirth and, broken-hearted, he too expired aged only 24.

The reins were then take up by Jamie Anderson of St Andrews and Bob Ferguson of Musselburgh. Each of them won the title three years in a row,

Anderson from 1877 to 1879 and Ferguson from 1880 to 1882 with the latter narrowly missing making it four in a row when he lost the Championship's first play-off in 1893 to Willie Fernie.

Scottish golfers continued to dominate the Championship over the next six years but with the field expanding annually it was only a matter of time before the tide was turned. In 1878 an English amateur, John Ball from Hoylake, had finished fifth when aged only 14, and 12 years later at Prestwick he made the important breakthrough. Ball's success was quickly emulated by another Hoylake amateur, Harold Hilton, who won in 1892 at Muirfield, the first time the Open was held over 72 holes and also the first time entry fees were levied. Prize money was trebled to more than £100.

The next significant milestone occurred in 1894 when the Championship was first staged in England. The Kentish links of St George's saw J. H. Taylor become the first English professional champion and this victory heralded a new era of domination as Taylor was joined by James Braid and Harry Vardon to form the Great Triumvirate. Between them they won the title 16 times in the space of 20 years with Vardon just edging out the five

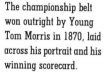

The championship belt won outright by Young Tom Morris in 1870, laid across his portrait and his winning scorecard.

Above J.H. Taylor playing in an exhibition match in 1908, and (left) James Braid at the 1902 Open Championship at Hoylake.

victories of the other two with his sixth win in 1914. Their influence was immeasurable with Vardon, in particular, bringing a new dimension to a game which hitherto had been one of crude lunge and bash. In 1898, Vardon became the first player to break 80 in all four rounds when he won at Prestwick, and the next target was to break 300 over the 72 holes. This honour fell to a little known English professional, Jack White from Sunningdale, whose last-round 69 in 1904 gave him a total of 296. This Championship also saw play being extended over three days, with the last two rounds on the final day, and the following year, in an attempt to ease the congestion created by more than 100 entrants, a qualifying figure of 15 strokes behind the leader after two rounds was introduced. This, in fact, only removed four players from the scene while 99 continued.

In 1907, Frenchman Arnaud Massy became the first overseas champion, winning at Hoylake, and four years later he nearly won again, tieing with Vardon at the now Royal St George's. The subsequent play-off ended in curious fashion with Massy picking up his ball on the 35th hole of the stroke-play encounter in deference to the fact that Vardon was several strokes ahead.

The reign of the Triumvirate came to an end with the outbreak of World War I and the suspension of the

Arnaud Massy, the first overseas Open Champion.

Harry Vardon, six times Open Champion.

Championship. Two pre-qualifying rounds were staged prior to the 1914 Open and the leading 80 players advanced to the Championship proper but it was becoming clear that the event needed administrative leadership. A letter from Herbert Fowler, architect of such courses at Walton Heath, Saunton and The Berkshire, advocated that since the R & A governed the rules of the game, it should also govern the game's most important championship.

The Great Triumvirate (left to right, Taylor, Braid and Vardon) with another great contemporary Sandy Herd (extreme right).

This came about in 1919 and the first Open under the R & A's jurisdiction was the first after the war, that of 1920 when George Duncan won at Deal. Duncan was nicknamed 'Miss 'em quick' because of the speed he executed each shot, an admirable philosophy but one which was to let him down two years later. By now the Championship had international appeal and in 1921 the old silver claret jug took the first of many subsequent journeys across the Atlantic when Jock Hutchison, a St Andrean who had emigrated to America, won at St Andrews after a play-off with amateur Roger Wethered. Wethered incurred a penalty stroke for inadvertently treading on his ball while walking backwards from studying the line of a shot in the third round. The Corinthian spirit of the amateur game in those days was exemplified by Wethered having to be persuaded to remain for the play-off because he felt that his commitment to a cricket match in England was more important!

The 1921 Championship saw the first appearance of Bobby Jones who tore up his card on the 11th hole, vowing never to return. Thankfully he did and over the next nine years he and Walter Hagen formed the spearhead of the American assault. Hagen broke through to win in 1922 at Royal St George's by one stroke from George Duncan who needed to get down in two from the hollow on the left of the 18th to tie. Duncan's quickness over the chip almost deceived the eye and he fluffed it.

Hagen, who was to win again in 1924, 1928 and 1929, epitomized the mood of the age. Flamboyantly dressed and darkly good-looking, he was the lounge lizard of the links. He lived life to the full, spending as he earned in the knowledge that another buck was always round the next corner. He had an ungainly, lunging swing but was a master of the short game and the chief exponent of rolling three shots into two.

In contrast, Jones was a quiet, somewhat introverted character who suffered nervous agonies during a championship but whose lovely, drowsy

The americanized Jock Hutchison who returned to his native St Andrews to take the 1921 Open Championship.

George Duncan chipping to the green during the 1923 Open at Troon.

swing rarely let him down. His first victory came at Royal Lytham and St Annes in 1926, the first time the Championship was staged there, and was notable for his legendary mashie shot from the scrubland to the left of the 17th in the final round. A plaque now marks the spot from where Jones struck that epic shot to completely demoralize his playing companion and nearest challenger, Al Watrous, although witnesses at the time now swear that the plaque is several yards out of place. Jones returned to St Andrews in 1927 and reconciled his relationship with the Old Course by setting a new record for the 72 holes of 285. Three years later he won again at Hoylake, on a much tighter rein this time due to a ridiculous seven at the 8th when he was by the green in two, fluffed a couple of chips and took three putts. This was the second leg of his Grand Slam and it earned him a ticker-tape welcome in New York on his return.

The only interlopers in the Hagen/Jones domination were Arthur Havers at Troon in 1923 and Jim Barnes at Prestwick in 1925, the latter being that

The flamboyant Walter Hagen.

Bobby Jones at St Andrews in 1927 where he retained his Open title.

A plaque on the 17th at Lytham marks the spot from which Bobby Jones launched his historic shot in 1926.

Henry Cotton on his way to victory at Sandwich, 1934.

Top Jim Barnes playing during the 1924 Open at Hoylake; he was to return a year later to take the title at Prestwick.

Top Alf Perry and (above) Alf Padgham, British winners of the Open in 1935 and 1936.

course's last Open due to its incapacity to cope with the crowds which swarmed across the links and effectively destroyed the hopes of Macdonald Smith who led by five strokes going into the last round but, swamped by the mob, crashed to an 82.

The American grip on the Championship continued in the new decade with Tommy Armour winning at Carnoustie in 1931, Gene Sarazen at Prince's, Sandwich in 1932 and Densmore Shute at St Andrews in 1933 after a play-off with fellow-American Craig Wood, the only man to lose a play-off in all four of the major professional Championships.

That dark time for British golf brought in a new dawn, however. Through sheer hard work and dedication, Henry Cotton had developed into a golfer whose striking was flawless. In 1934 at Royal St George's he converted that control into the two lowest opening rounds the Championship had ever seen, or has ever seen since. His first round was 67 and he looked like matching that in the second except that he finished with two threes for a 65, a score of such historic lowness that it gave birth to probably the most famous golf ball of them all, the Dunlop 65. His third round of 72 left him ten strokes clear of the field and a new record aggregate looked likely. But prior to the final round he was assailed by stomach cramps and eventually limped home with a 79, still good enough to give him victory by five strokes and tie the lowest aggregate score of 283 that Sarazen had set two years earlier.

Cotton's victory gave Britain a national hero and ushered in an unprecedented spell of home triumphs. The little known Alf Perry won at Muirfield the next year, hitting woods out of bunkers like a man in a weekend

68

knockabout, Alf Padgham won at Hoylake in 1936, the year he swept all before him, and then it was Cotton's turn again. Carnoustie in 1937 saw the full might of the victorious American Ryder Cup team assembled, but with another display of sublime striking Cotton produced a final round of 71 over the rain-lashed links to win by two strokes over Reg Whitcombe. The latter became the man of the moment at Royal St George's in 1938 when he stood foursquare in the tempest which swept the links to win by one shot from James Adams, who had also been runner-up to Padgham in 1936. In 1939, at St Andrews, Dick Burton unwittingly became the Champion who was to hold the title for the longest spell due to the more pressing matters of World War II.

The Championship resumed in 1946 at St Andrews when German POWs helped to prepare the course. The story goes that Sam Snead was travelling there by train in company with a bucolic Brigadier and, glancing out of the window, Snead remarked that he thought he saw an old, disused golf course. 'That, Sir,' spluttered his companion, 'is the Old Course at St Andrews!' Snead, no respecter of reputations, added insult to injury by winning the first prize of £150 by four strokes. Ulster's Fred Daly became the first Irish winner in 1947 at Hoylake, and he was followed by Cotton who took his third title at Muirfield and laid on a second round of 66 in front of King George VI.

The Championship now entered an era that could loosely be described as the age of the Commonwealth. In fact, it was a ten-year period of domination by two players, Bobby Locke of South Africa and Peter Thomson of Australia. Between them they won the title eight times in that spell with only Max Faulkner (1951) and Ben Hogan (1953) breaking the sequence. Locke was extremely unorthodox, hitting every shot over cover point and bringing the ball back on target, but as a putter he had few equals and this coupled with an imperturbable temperament made him a fearsome competitor. His first victory came at

Bobby Locke (left) and Harry Bradshaw shake hands after the final round which left them tied in the 1949 Open.

Royal St George's in 1949 when he defeated Ireland's Harry Bradshaw after a play-off. This was the Championship when Bradshaw hit his drive to the 5th during the second round and the ball finished in a broken beer bottle. Unsure of his rights, he elected to play the ball and the hole cost him a seven and 77 for the round. Locke repeated his victory at Troon the following year and became the first man to break 280 for the 72 holes.

Royal Portrush became the only Irish Club to stage the Open in 1951 when Max Faulkner managed to win despite tempting the fates by signing autographs as 'Open Champion' before he went out for the last round. Locke won again at Royal Lytham and St Annes in 1952 and then it was 1953, the year Ben Hogan bestrode the world. He arrived at Carnoustie a week early and plotted a path to the title in relentless fashion. Rounds of

73, 71, 70 and 68 in ascending order of brilliance sealed his place among the immortals and made him the only professional to win three Majors in a single year.

Peter Thomson won the first of his hat-trick of titles in 1954 at Royal Birkdale. A master tactician, Thomson's strength lay in accurate driving coupled with an astute golfing brain, qualities which have since held him in good stead on the US Seniors Tour. His victory in 1955 earned him the first £1,000 winner's cheque and in 1956 he became the fourth man in Open history to win three in a row. The 1957 Open was switched from Muirfield to St Andrews because of the Suez crisis and petrol rationing and Locke won from Thomson. The two were not exactly bosom pals and controversy arose when, on the final green, Locke marked his ball and moved the marker a putter-head's length away to allow his partner to putt. He then replaced his ball without moving the marker back to the original spot, and holed out. After much deliberation, the Committee decided that Locke's score should stand since he had gained no advantage. There was a chance of a British victory in 1958 at Lytham when David Thomas tied with Thomson but it was not to be as Thomson won the play-off by four strokes. The end of the decade saw Gary Player perform the first of his miraculous recoveries when he made up eight strokes over the last two rounds at Muirfield to win, despite taking six on the final hole.

Australia's Kel Nagle secured a popular victory in the 1960 Centenary Open at St Andrews but this Championship is perhaps best remembered for the dynamic presence of Arnold Palmer. The man who had taken American golf by the scruff of the neck was about to do the same for the Open. He finished second to Nagle by a single stroke on his first appearance but was not to be denied at Birkdale in 1961 when he powered his way through some of the foulest weather imaginable to win by a stroke from Dai Rees, the irrepressible Welshman who had also been runner-up in 1953 and 1954. Palmer put the field to

flight in 1962 at Troon over a course that was baked hard by a prolonged dry spell, winning by six strokes and setting a new Championship record of 276 for 72 holes. It was also the first appearance of Jack Nicklaus who only just qualified for the last two rounds.

Led by Palmer, the American challenge was now in full cry. Bob Charles halted it in 1963 at Lytham when he became the first left-hander and the first New Zealander to win as he out-putted America's Phil Rodgers in a play-off, but 1964 at St Andrews saw one of the most remarkable victories in recent times. Tony Lema arrived at the Old Course with only enough time for one full practice round; his style and elegance captured not only the hearts of the spectators but also the title, by five strokes from Nicklaus. Peter Thomson took the fifth and most satisfying of his Opens at Birkdale in 1965 against the full might of the American invasion and then Nicklaus, after near-misses in 1963 and 1964, finally broke through at Muirfield in 1966 over a course whose rough was formidably high.

Hoylake in 1967 witnessed one of the most popular victories when, after 19 years of trying, Roberto de Vicenzo held off Nicklaus to win. Unfortunately the size of the crowds sounded the death knell for Hoylake as an Open venue. Gary Player took his second Open at Carnoustie in 1968 after a thrilling battle with the ubiquitous Nicklaus and then came the spark that ignited the first European golf explosion.

Eighteen years without a British victory had left the populace hungry for a hero. It found him in Tony Jacklin, a player who had won in America the previous year, and who had the charisma and personality to accompany an aggressive mode of play. At Lytham in 1969 he ended the British drought of victories with a two-stroke margin over Bob Charles and launched himself into the hearts of millions. A year later, Jacklin also won the US Open, an unprecedented feat by an Englishman, but the next three Opens saw fate deal him some of the cruellest hands in Open history. In 1970 at St Andrews, Jacklin covered the first

Above Peter Thomson enjoys the attention of the Press after his first Open win in 1954.

Right David Thomas in the lead at Lytham at the end of the third round in 1958.

Above Peter Alliss sinks his final putt at St Andrews during the 1960 Centenary Open to break the course record.

Left Bob Charles, whose immaculate putting destroyed Phil Rodgers in the 1963 play-off.

Jack Nicklaus shows the details of the final round at Muirfield which won him his first Open title in 1966.

Above Tony Jacklin on his way to the Open Championship title in 1969 and (left) the first Englishman to hold the trophy for eighteen years.

Far left Jack Nicklaus throws his putter in the air to celebrate his win at the end of the play-off in 1970 but nearly flattens the luckless Doug Sanders in the process.

Above Mr Lu congratulates Lee Trevino on his first Open victory at Birkdale in 1971 and (left) Trevino pitches stone dead at the 10th on his way to a second win at Muirfield the following year.

nine holes of the opening round in 29 strokes and he appeared set to break all kinds of records before a thunderstorm halted play. The next day the magic had gone and although he finished with a 67, it was a question of what might have been as Jack Nicklaus and Doug Sanders tied after 72 holes. Sanders had pre-qualified for the Championship and performed magnificently to come to the final hole needing a par four for victory. In an agonizing sequence of indecision he contrived to take five, ultimately missing a putt of three feet to avoid the play-off which Nicklaus won. In 1971, Jacklin gallantly harassed Lee Trevino at Birkdale but there was no stopping the American as he added the Open to the US and Canadian Opens he had won in the previous two weeks. Trevino's defeat of Jacklin in the 1972 Open at Muirfield was a tragedy for the Englishman. In the third round Trevino holed a chip and a bunker shot which struck the pin halfway up and dropped, and then in the last round on the 71st hole he chipped in again just when Jacklin looked as though he would take the lead. The events at Muirfield signalled the end of Jacklin as an Open challenger.

The tall, soldierly figure of Tom Weiskopf marched to victory at rain-sodden Troon in 1973 and then Gary Player became the only man to win the Open in three different decades when he led from start to finish in 1974 at Lytham, the first Open when the large ball was made compulsory. Carnoustie in 1975 saw the beginning of Tom Watson's domination as he captured the title five times in nine years. He defeated Australia's Jack Newton in a play-off in 1975 and then went on to win at Turnberry in 1977, Muirfield in 1980, Troon in 1982 and Birkdale in 1983. His battle with Nicklaus at Turnberry was an epic as the two of them went at each other like bare-knuckle prize-fighters over the final 36 holes. Playing together, nothing separated them until Watson birdied the 71st hole and Nicklaus didn't. Watson's aggregate of 268 was eight strokes better than the previous one set by Palmer and Weiskopf at Troon in 1962 and 1973 respectively.

The Watson period also saw the emergence of Severiano Ballesteros who first captivated audiences with his audacious play at Birkdale in 1976 when he led after three rounds. Slashing his way through Birkdale's dunes, Ballesteros finally succumbed to Johnny Miller's greater experience but his hour was not long in coming. Following Nicklaus's third Open at St Andrews in 1978,

Tom Watson and Jack Nicklaus wait among the rocks at the 9th for play to resume during their epic duel at Turnberry in 1977.

Jack Nicklaus addresses the crowd after being presented with the Open trophy in 1978. Peter Oosterhuis on his right (yellow sweater) and Simon Owen on his left (red trousers) reflect on what might have been.

Ballesteros thrust himself to the centre of the world stage with a cavalier performance at Lytham in 1979. Rarely on the fairway, the young Spaniard overhauled the third-round leader, Hale Irwin, to become the first Continental winner since Arnaud Massy in 1907 and started a new European golf explosion.

In 1981 the Championship returned to Royal St George's after an

Seve bursts through the crowd on his way to victory in the 1979 Open at Lytham.

absence of 32 years and America's Bill Rogers won handily; the growing European strength was emphasized by Bernhard Langer finishing runner-up. Watson won at Troon in 1982 after Zimbabwe's Nick Price squandered a three-stroke lead with six holes to play and the chunky American won again at Birkdale in 1983, hitting a superlative 2-iron to the final green to win by a stroke from Americans Andy Bean and Hale Irwin, the latter having suffered an inexplicable lapse in the third round when he went to tap in a one-inch putt and missed the ball altogether.

Now sitting on a hat-trick and with a chance to equal Harry Vardon's record of six Open titles, Watson came to St Andrews in 1984 as clear favourite. A little-known Australian, Ian Baker-Finch, made the early running but the final round developed into an intense struggle between Watson, Ballesteros and, to a slightly lesser extent, Langer. The climax came at the infamous Road Hole, the 17th, where Ballesteros made a par four and Watson, playing immediately behind, was betrayed by that same 2-iron which earned him victory the previous year. His second shot with that club to the 17th flew over the green to finish up against the wall, and while Watson was taking five Ballesteros was clinching victory with a birdie three on the last green. Record crowds of 187,753 attended during the week and prize-money was raised to £451,000.

The £500,000 barrier was broken in 1985 when Royal St George's was the venue for the second time in five years. The extraordinary talents of Sandy Lyle, who had played three rounds of the Open as a 16-year-old schoolboy in 1974, finally came to fruition as he grabbed a title nobody seemed to want to win by dint of two birdies over the final five holes. Lyle's victory ended a 16-year barren period of British wins and earned him £65,000 compared with the £4,250 Jacklin won in 1969. Turnberry got the nod again in 1986 and the way the course was set up showed that the Championship Committee were keen on preventing any repeats of the 1977 low-scoring Watson/

Another long putt goes in for Sandy Lyle during the closing holes of the final round at Royal St George's in 1985.

Nicklaus spectacular. The Committee need not really have bothered since the weather did the job pretty effectively. High winds and lashing rain squalls found most of the field struggling in the thick, cloying rough. But no matter what the examination paper, one student always seems to have the answers and in this case it was Greg Norman, in the midst of his *annus mirabilis,* who, in the second round, nearly scored 100 per cent. Norman fired a 63 in that round to tie the Championship record set by Mark Hayes in 1977 and Isao Aoki in 1980. Norman could have set a new record but for three-putting the final green; his score for the round gave him a lead he never relinquished. In 1987 Nick Faldo provided Britain with its second home victory in three years when he completed his final round with 18 consecutive pars, an unprecedented feat in the history of the Championship. The victory earned Faldo £75,000 – not the largest prize in world golf in these inflated times but one which every competitor would give their eye teeth to win, for the title of 'Champion Golfer of the Year' means an elevation to immortality.

A winner at last! Greg Norman with the Open trophy at Turnberry in 1986.

THE OPEN CHAMPIONSHIP
The Belt

Year	Winner	Country	Score	Venue
1860	W Park	GB	174	Prestwick
1861	T Morris, sen	GB	163	Prestwick
1862	T Morris, sen	GB	163	Prestwick
1863	W Park	GB	168	Prestwick
1864	T Morris, sen	GB	167	Prestwick
1865	A Strath	GB	162	Prestwick
1866	W Park	GB	169	Prestwick
1867	T Morris, sen	GB	170	Prestwick
1868	T Morris, jun	GB	157	Prestwick
1869	T Morris, jun	GB	154	Prestwick
1870	T Morris, jun	GB	149	Prestwick

The Cup

Year	Winner	Country	Score	Venue
1872	T Morris, jun	GB	166	Prestwick
1873	T Kidd	GB	179	St Andrews
1874	M Park	GB	159	Musselburgh
1875	W Park	GB	166	Prestwick
1876	R Martin	GB	176	St Andrews
1877	J Anderson	GB	160	Musselburgh
1878	J Anderson	GB	157	Prestwick
1879	J Anderson	GB	169	St Andrews
1880	R Ferguson	GB	162	Musselburgh
1881	R Ferguson	GB	170	Prestwick
1882	R Ferguson	GB	171	St Andrews
1883	W Fernie	GB	159	Musselburgh
1884	J Simpson	GB	160	Prestwick
1885	R Martin	GB	171	St Andrews
1886	D Brown	GB	157	Musselburgh
1887	W Park, jun	GB	161	Prestwick
1888	J Burns	GB	171	St Andrews
1889	W Park, jun	GB	155	Musselburgh
1890	J Ball (Am)	GB	164	Prestwick
1891	H Kirkaldy	GB	166	St Andrews

After 1891 the competition was extended to 72 holes

Year	Winner	Country	Score	Venue
1892	H Hilton (Am)	GB	305	Muirfield
1893	W Auchterlonie	GB	322	Prestwick
1894	JH Taylor	GB	326	Sandwich
1895	JH Taylor	GB	322	St Andrews
1896	H Vardon	GB	316	Muirfield
1897	H Hilton (Am)	GB	314	Hoylake
1898	H Vardon	GB	307	Prestwick
1899	H Vardon	GB	310	Sandwich
1900	JH Taylor	GB	309	St Andrews
1901	J Braid	GB	309	Muirfield
1902	A Herd	GB	307	Hoylake
1903	H Vardon	GB	300	Prestwick
1904	J White	GB	296	Sandwich
1905	J Braid	GB	318	St Andrews
1906	J Braid	GB	300	Muirfield
1907	A Massy	France	312	Hoylake
1908	J Braid	GB	291	Prestwick
1909	JH Taylor	GB	295	Deal
1910	J Braid	GB	299	St Andrews
1911	H Vardon	GB	303	Sandwich
1912	E Ray	GB	295	Muirfield
1913	JH Taylor	GB	304	Hoylake
1914	H Vardon	GB	306	Prestwick
1915-19	No Championship			
1920	G Duncan	GB	303	Deal
1921	J Hutchison	USA	296	St Andrews
1922	W Hagen	USA	300	Sandwich
1923	AG Havers	GB	295	Troon
1924	W Hagen	USA	301	Hoylake
1925	J Barnes	USA	300	Prestwick
1926	R Jones, jun (Am)	USA	291	Lytham and St. Annes

Year	Winner	Country	Score	Venue
1927	R Jones, jun (Am)	USA	285	St Andrews
1928	W Hagen	USA	292	Sandwich
1929	W Hagen	USA	292	Muirfield
1930	R Jones, jun (Am)	USA	291	Hoylake
1931	T Armour	USA	296	Carnoustie
1932	G Sarazen	USA	283	Prince's, Sandwich
1933	D Shute	USA	292	St Andrews
1934	H Cotton	GB	283	Sandwich
1935	A Perry	GB	283	Muirfield
1936	A Padgham	GB	287	Hoylake
1937	H Cotton	GB	290	Carnoustie
1938	R Whitcombe	GB	295	Sandwich
1939	R Burton	GB	290	St Andrews
1940-45	No Championship			
1946	S Snead	USA	290	St Andrews
1947	F Daly	GB	293	Hoylake
1948	H Cotton	GB	284	Muirfield
1949	AD Locke	South Africa	283	Sandwich
1950	AD Locke	South Africa	279	Troon
1951	M Faulkner	GB	285	Portrush
1952	AD Locke	South Africa	287	Lytham and St Annes
1953	B Hogan	USA	282	Carnoustie
1954	P Thomson	Australia	283	Birkdale
1955	P Thomson	Australia	281	St Andrews
1956	P Thomson	Australia	286	Hoylake
1957	AD Locke	South Africa	279	St Andrews
1958	P Thomson	Australia	278	Lytham and St Annes
1959	G Player	South Africa	284	Muirfield
1960	K Nagle	Australia	278	St Andrews
1961	A Palmer	USA	284	Birkdale
1962	A Palmer	USA	276	Troon
1963	R Charles	New Zealand	277	Lytham and St Annes
1964	T Lema	USA	279	St Andrews
1965	P Thomson	Australia	285	Birkdale
1966	J Nicklaus	USA	282	Muirfield
1967	R De Vicenzo	Argentine	278	Hoylake
1968	G Player	South Africa	289	Carnoustie
1969	A Jacklin	GB	280	Lytham and St Annes
1970	J Nicklaus	USA	283	St Andrews
1971	L Trevino	USA	278	Birkdale
1972	L Trevino	USA	278	Muirfield
1973	T Weiskopf	USA	276	Troon
1974	G Player	South Africa	282	Lytham and St Annes
1975	T Watson	USA	279	Carnoustie
1976	J Miller	USA	279	Birkdale
1977	T Watson	USA	268	Turnberry
1978	J Nicklaus	USA	281	St Andrews
1979	S Ballesteros	Spain	283	Lytham and St Annes
1980	T Watson	USA	271	Muirfield
1981	W Rogers	USA	276	Sandwich
1982	T Watson	USA	284	Troon
1983	T Watson	USA	275	Birkdale
1984	S Ballesteros	Spain	276	St Andrews
1985	S Lyle	GB	282	Sandwich
1986	G Norman	Australia	280	Turnberry
1987	N Faldo	GB	279	Muirfield

THE MASTERS

In a country whose history is measured in centuries rather than aeons, tradition is a prized commodity. Thus it is that American golf has latched onto the Masters tournament as being a tangible link with the past, solely because of the event's creator, Bobby Jones. It was Jones who demonstrated the qualities of sportsmanship coupled with a playing record that has no parallel and when he retired from competitive golf to build his own course and start his own tournament, American golf had tradition thrust upon it.

These are the credentials which have made the Masters a major championship, although the Augusta National Club which stages and organizes it does not refer to the event as a championship but simply as a tournament. That may be regarded as inverted snobbery but it is all part of the Club's philosophy of running the tightest ship in world golf. For a start, the Masters is not an open tournament. Players qualify to play through various successes but still have to receive an invitation. Tickets are limited and cannot be bought at the gate but are handed down from generation to generation. There is no advertising on the course and no tournament programme. The atmosphere at the Masters is one of genteel Southern hospitality that is fiercely protected by a steely, quiet authority. Above all, the Masters is a week for the players. They play in twos rather than the more general three-ball pairings, the crowds never spill over onto the fairways and the course is prepared to such an extent that even the water in the hazards is dyed blue.

The glories of Augusta are more fully described in the chapter on courses but, suffice to say, the course's design is such that it has inspired some of the most heroic, breath-taking and stunning finishes in the history of the game. From Horton Smith, winning the first Masters in 1934, to Larry Mize's holed chip in 1987, the tournament has always drawn out something extra from each winner's repertoire of strokes.

The first resounding shot came in 1935 when Gene Sarazen stood in the middle of the par-five 15th needing three birdies to tie with Craig Wood. He disposed of that requirement by the simple expedient of hitting his 4-wood second shot straight into the hole for an albatross two. Sarazen won the play-off to become the first professional to win all four major titles. The pattern of dramatic

Above The plaque at Augusta to commemorate Gene Sarazen's amazing shot with a 4-wood at the 15th.

Left The well-protected entrance to the Augusta National Club.

turnarounds continued over the next two years when, in 1936, Horton Smith made up six strokes on Harry Cooper to win for the second time, and in 1937 Byron Nelson played the 12th and 13th in two and three while the leader, Ralph Guldahl, played them in five and six. Guldahl finished second again in 1938 to Henry Picard but took the honours in 1939. The Masters continued well into World War II with Jimmy Demaret winning in 1940 and Craig Wood making amends for previous disappointments in 1941. Byron Nelson and Ben Hogan tied in 1942 and the play-off produced a scintillating spell of scoring from Nelson who trailed by three strokes after five holes but then overhauled Hogan to win by one stroke.

It seemed that Hogan was never to win the Masters for when it resumed in 1946 after a break due to the war, he three-putted the final green to lose by a stroke to Herman Keiser. But Hogan, and also Sam Snead, were both too accomplished to be denied the title for much longer. Demaret joined Smith and Nelson as double winners in 1947 and in 1948 Claude Harmon set a new record aggregate of 279; then it was the turn of Snead and Hogan. Between them, over the next six years, they won five times with only Demaret interruping the sequence with his third win in 1950. Snead won in 1949, 1952 and 1954, the latter after a play-off with Hogan, while Hogan won in 1951 and 1953, the year he was virtually unbeatable. The 1954 Masters was notable for the excitement created by amateur Billy Joe Patton who holed-in-one at the 6th to take the lead on the final day, but he came to watery grief at the 13th and finished one stroke out of the play-off.

Amateur representation at the Masters has always been a feature, but no amateur has ever won. Following Cary Middlecoff's comfortable seven-stroke win in 1955, it looked as though an amateur would win in 1956 as Ken Venturi stood four strokes clear after 54 holes. A combination of nerves and a blustery wind got the better of him and he stumbled to a last-round 80 as Jack Burke made up an eight-stroke deficit to win. Speedy Doug Ford, a player who often holed out before his partners had even reached the green, whipped in a last-round 66 to win in 1957 but the time had now come for the Masters to be hauled into the limelight of one man's charisma.

Above Byron Nelson still playing in the Masters in 1962, twenty years after his memorable play-off with Ben Hogan.

Left Jack Burke, Masters Champion in 1956.

The Augusta pines echoed to the cries of 'Charge!' as Arnold Palmer made it his habit to win and lose the title in alternate years. The broad fairways and tantalizing pin positions eminently suited Palmer's attacking style as he won in 1958, 1960, 1962 and 1964. In between, his instincts betrayed him as he lost out in 1959 to Art Wall who fired five birdies in the last six holes for a 66; in 1961 to Gary Player, a most memorable collapse when Palmer took six at the final hole from a greenside bunker when a four would have brought victory, and in 1963 to Jack Nicklaus who caused further consternation in 'Arnie's Army' by taking the first of his six Masters. Nicklaus's second win was not far away either, for in 1965 he obliterated the field to win by nine strokes from Player and Palmer in a scoring exhibition (67, 71, 64, 69 – 271) that prompted Bobby Jones to comment that the winner played a game with which Jones was not familiar.

Now the joint holder of the lowest round and also the lowest aggregate, Nicklaus set another record in 1966 by becoming the first player to win in successive years when he defeated Gay Brewer and Tommy Jacobs in a play-off. Brewer's loopy swing did the business properly in 1967, and then came the Masters the Augusta committee would rather forget. Bob Goalby was the winner but the tragedy centred upon Roberto de Vicenzo. The Argentinian finished his final round with what he thought was a 65 and, mobbed by excited well-wishers, signed his card without really checking it. He failed to notice that his marker, Tommy Aaron, who was to win in 1973, had put down a four on the 17th when the world had witnessed the Argentinian make a birdie three. The higher score had to stand and de Vicenzo's restated 66 left him one stroke behind Goalby. The next year a small tent was erected at the back of the 18th for players to attend to their scorecards in peace.

At 6 ft 6 in (1.98 m), George Archer became the tallest Masters winner in 1969 to be followed by Billy Casper in 1970, after a play-off with Gene Littler, and by Charles Coody in 1971. Nicklaus

equalled Palmer's record of four victories in 1972 and Tommy Aaron won in 1973, the year when Britain's Peter Oosterhuis went into a rain-delayed final round with a three-stroke lead but could only manage a 74 to Aaron's closing 68. Gary Player took his second Masters in 1974, a 9-iron

second to within inches of the hole on the 71st hole being the decisive stroke.

Now the Masters moved up an extra gear with a series of thrilling finishes. In 1975, Nicklaus was locked in a titanic struggle with Tom Weiskopf and Johnny Miller over the closing holes and it was a putt of 45 feet by Nicklaus on the 16th green which edged him a stroke ahead. Arriving on the final green, Miller and Weiskopf both had putts to tie but missed.

Nobody could live with Ray

Jack Nicklaus at Augusta in 1972, about to equal Arnold Palmer's record of four victories.

Above Tom Watson helps Gary Player into his third green jacket in 1978.

Right After many narrow misses Ben Crenshaw eventually wins his first major at Augusta in 1984.

The few millimetres by which Ed Sneed missed the Masters title in 1979.

Floyd in 1976 as he opened with rounds of 65 and 66 and ended eight strokes clear, equalling Nicklaus's record aggregate of 271. Tom Watson confronted Nicklaus over the final nine holes in 1977 and withstood the pressure to win by two strokes, and then Gary Player wrote another unbelievable chapter in Masters history. Seven strokes behind leader Hubert Green with ten holes to play, Player birdied seven of those holes for a round of 64 to set a target only Green could match. On the final hole Green faced a putt of around three feet to tie but missed to make the South African the oldest winner at that time. More drama occurred in 1979 when Ed Sneed squandered a three-stroke lead with three holes left to play to end in a tie with Tom Watson and Fuzzy Zoeller. It was the first sudden-death play-off and Zoeller won it on the second extra hole to become the first to win, apart from inaugural winner Horton Smith, at his first attempt.

Following his victory in the 1979 Open, Severiano Ballesteros had been branded a slasher by the Americans, but exhibiting a controlled and fluid swing he laid waste to Augusta in 1980 to establish a ten-stroke lead with just nine holes to play. He stumbled on the homeward run to see that lead evaporate to two strokes but pulled himself together to become the second overseas player to win after Player, the first European winner and, at 23, the youngest. After Tom Watson and Craig Stadler won in 1981 and 1982, Ballesteros secured his second win in 1983. The

Spaniard trailed by one stroke at the start of the final round but an eagle and two birdies in the first four holes put the rest of the field to flight. Frequently a runner-up in major championships, Ben Crenshaw finally put his name on one when he putted quite beautifully in 1984 to win by two strokes from Tom Watson.

European golf was given further impetus in 1985 when West Germany's Bernhard Langer took advantage of some costly errors from Curtis Strange over the last nine holes to win. Ballesteros finished second.

As long as golf is played, the events of the 1986 Masters will be remembered. American golf was smarting from the loss of the Ryder Cup and the fact that Sandy Lyle had won the Open and Langer was the defending Masters champion. It needed a new hero. Instead it had to fall back on an old one as Jack Nicklaus came through with a final round of 65 to hold off the challenge of Greg Norman and Ballesteros. Ballesteros looked a likely winner when he eagled the 13th with a searing second shot to the green but he struck an uncharacteristically awful second shot to the 15th into the water and his challenge was sunk. Norman needed a par four at the final hole to tie but put his second into the crowd on the right to finish in second place along with a perennial Masters runner-up, Tom Kite, who missed a shortish birdie putt to tie. The victory made Nicklaus, at 46, the oldest winner and his sixth Masters gave him a total of 20 major championships including two US Amateur titles.

In the modern game there has been no player to equal Nicklaus, and it is entirely appropriate that his latest major title, one hesitates to say his last, should occur at the shrine of Bobby Jones, indisputably the greatest player of a previous era.

The Masters provides a standard of excellence that is rarely matched anywhere else in the world. For golfers everywhere, the Masters heralds the start of a new season and as long as the azaleas and dogwoods continue to bloom round Augusta National, that feeling of anticipation will remain.

Jack Nicklaus wins his sixth Masters title in 1986, twenty-three years after his first green jacket.

US MASTERS' CHAMPIONSHIP
Played every year at Augusta National Golf Course

Year	Winner	Country	Score	Year	Winner	Country	Score
1934	H Smith	USA	284	1963	J Nicklaus	USA	286
1935	G Sarazen	USA	282	1964	A Palmer	USA	276
1936	H Smith	USA	285	1965	J Nicklaus	USA	271
1937	B Nelson	USA	283	1966	J Nicklaus	USA	288
1938	H Pickard	USA	285	1967	G Brewer	USA	280
1939	R Guldahl	USA	279	1968	R Goalby	USA	277
1940	J Demaret	USA	280	1969	G Archer	USA	281
1941	C Wood	USA	280	1970	W Casper	USA	279
1942	B Nelson	USA	280	1971	C Coody	USA	279
1946	H Keiser	USA	282	1972	J Nicklaus	USA	286
1947	J Demaret	USA	281	1973	T Aaron	USA	283
1948	C Harmon	USA	279	1974	G Player	South Africa	278
1949	S Snead	USA	283	1975	J Nicklaus	USA	276
1950	J Demaret	USA	282	1976	R Floyd	USA	271
1951	B Hogan	USA	280	1977	T Watson	USA	276
1952	S Snead	USA	286	1978	G Player	South Africa	277
1953	B Hogan	USA	274	1979	F Zoeller	USA	280
1954	S Snead	USA	289	1980	S Ballesteros	Spain	275
1955	C Middlecoff	USA	279	1981	T Watson	USA	280
1956	J Burke	USA	289	1982	C Stadler	USA	284
1957	D Ford	USA	283	1983	S Ballesteros	Spain	280
1958	A Palmer	USA	284	1984	B Crenshaw	USA	277
1959	A Wall	USA	284	1985	B Langer	W. Germany	278
1960	A Palmer	USA	282	1986	J Nicklaus	USA	279
1961	G Player	South Africa	280	1987	L Mize	USA	285
1962	A Palmer	USA	280				

US OPEN

Golf was still in its infancy in America when the first United States Open Championship was staged in 1894. The American Amateur had been held a year earlier as a match-play event, and the US Open followed suit. It was won by Willie Dunn by two holes over W. Campbell at St Andrews, New York.

The Championship became stroke-play the following year and it is generally acknowledged that the winner, Horace Rawlins, was the first US Open Champion. It was played over the nine-hole course at Newport, Rhode Island and Rawlins, a British emigrant, set the pattern for a series of victories by British-born players.

It was not until 1900 that the title was won by an overseas player. This was Harry Vardon who won by two strokes over J.H. Taylor at Wheaton, Chicago. Vardon and Taylor were engaged on a year-long tour of America at the time, spreading the gospel of golf to an enthusiastic public. Four of the next five years were the preserve of Willie Anderson, another Scottish-born resident, and his hat-trick of victories (1903–05) has never been matched although Bobby Jones, Ben Hogan and Jack Nicklaus joined Anderson with four wins apiece. Still the Scots dominated as Alex Smith, brother of Macdonald Smith, won twice in 1906 and 1910. Then in 1911 America had its first home-bred winner when Johnny McDermott won at Wheaton and again the next year at Buffalo.

The shock waves of the next Championship are still reverberating round the world. The Country Club at Brookline, Mass., saw Vardon and Ted Ray looking set to take the title back to Britain again as they tied for first place. They were joined, however, by a young amateur, Francis Ouimet, and in the biggest upset in the game at that time Ouimet beat them both in the play-off; the graph of American golf was set to continue its upward path.

Home players took up the reins with Walter Hagen winning in 1914 and 1919 and amateurs Jerome Travers and

Charles Evans taking the two titles prior to suspension of the Championship for World War I. The 1920 Championship was significant not so much for the victory by Ray, the last Englishman to win until Tony Jacklin in 1970, but for the first appearance of the 18-year-old Georgia prodigy, Bobby Jones. Jones finished eighth that year at Inverness, Ohio, which was the first club to open its doors to professionals, a gesture which prompted Hagen to make a collection among his fellows to present a grandfather clock which now stands in the main lobby bearing the message:
'God measures men by what they are
Not what they in wealth possess
This vibrant message chimes afar
The voice of Inverness'

The first of Jones's four victories did not come until two years later, Jim Barnes and Gene Sarazen interceding, but after his initial win in 1923 he never finished lower than second in seven attempts with the wins coming in 1926, 1929 and 1930 – a record of staggering consistency. His final and most important win came at Interlachen when he made three birdies in the last five holes to edge home by a stroke and complete the third leg of his Impregnable Quadrilateral.

By 1931 the prize fund had risen to over $2,000 and that year's Championship at Inverness produced a unique play-off marathon between Billy Burke and George von Elm. Tied after 72 holes, they were still locked after 36 more and had to play yet another 36 before Burke ended a stroke in front. In 1932 Flushing Meadow, New York was the site of a remarkable spell of scoring by Gene Sarazen who came from seven strokes behind, playing the last 28 holes in exactly 100 strokes: a two at the ninth in the third round, a 32 home and a final 66. It made Sarazen the second man after Jones to win two Opens in one year and his aggregate of 286 tied the record set by Evans in 1916.

Jones having departed the scene in 1930, amateurs were becoming less of a force and Johnny Goodman's victory in 1933 remains the last time an amateur

Right John McDermott, the first American-born professional to win the US Open.

Right Francis Ouimet playing in the Amateur Championship at Sandwich the year after his US Open victory in 1913 and (below right) Charles Evans, another American amateur who won the US Open title in 1916.

Far right Gene Sarazen (left) and Bobby Jones (right), winners of the US Open in 1922 and 1923 respectively.

Above Julius Boros, two-time winner of the US Open, and (right) Tommy Bolt, winner in 1958 and notorious for his temperamental behaviour.

Top Lawson Little and (far right) Lloyd Mangrum, both US Open winners after play-offs in 1940 and 1946.

triumphed. Olin Dutra, Tony Manero and Ralph Guldahl (twice) won over the next four years with Guldahl's victory in 1937 setting new 72-hole record of 281.

The most quoted fact about Sam Snead is that he was the best player never to win the US Open but this should not detract from his status as one of the great figures in the game. Nonetheless, he never did win the title and his performance on the last hole at Spring Mill, Philadelphia in 1939 was enough to scar a man for life. Standing on the last tee, Snead needed a par five to win although he thought he needed a birdie four. Gambling on hitting the green with his second shot he instead found a plugged lie in a bunker and on reaching the green in five shots, three-putted for an eight. It was one of the most notorious collapses in golf and Snead did not even get into the play-off between Byron Nelson, Craig Wood and Densmore Shute which Nelson won for his sole US Open title.

Lawson Little and Craig Wood completed the list of winners prior to World War II and on the Championship's return in 1946 at Canterbury, Ohio, the prize-money had climbed to $8,000. Lloyd Mangrum, a veteran of the Normandy landings and winner of the Purple Heart, outlasted Nelson and Vic Ghezzi in the play-off to take the first prize of $1,500. Snead was the victim of some gamesmanship in 1947 when he tied with Lew Worsham at St Louis, Missouri. On the final green the two were still tied and both balls lay almost equidistant from the hole. Snead was about to putt from around three feet when Worsham stepped forward to query whether it was in fact Snead's turn to play. It transpired it was, but Snead, obviously disturbed by the interruption, missed and Worsham holed.

Ben Hogan won the first of his four titles at Riviera, Los Angeles in 1948, smashing the Championship record in the process with a score of 276, but was unable to defend in 1949 because of a horrific car accident which almost cost him his life and put him in hospital for nearly a year. Cary Middlecoff stepped into the breach with Snead once again second. Hogan returned in 1950 and,

though hardly able to walk due to his extensive injuries, hauled himself round Merion to tie with Mangrum and George Fazio. His 2-iron second to the final hole of the 72 has become part of the game's legend. And he won the play-off. The legend continued in 1951 at Oakland Hills when Hogan destroyed one of the toughest courses in the Championship's history with a final round of 67. The course had been specifically made harder by architect Robert Trent Jones and the players decried it to a man. At the end of his final round Hogan, not noted for his quotability, made the memorable comment: 'I'm glad I brought this course, this monster, to its knees.'

Julius Boros interrupted the Hogan sequence in 1952 but the little man from Texas had no peers in 1953 as he won at Oakmont to make it three major titles for the year. Following Ed Furgol's win at Baltusrol in 1954, the question on everybody's lips was: could Hogan capture a record fifth US Open at Olympic, San Francisco? It seemed he could when he finished the 72 holes with only the unknown Jack Fleck still on the course with a chance. Unperturbed by the moment, Fleck coolly holed a putt of seven feet on the final green to tie. The legacy of his accident was taking its toll on Hogan's legs and, although he stood only one stroke behind on the 18th tee of the play-off, his foot slipped on the drive and his ball finished deep in the rough. Hogan finished with a flourish by holing a long putt for a six but Fleck had won the day.

That, however, was not to be Hogan's last challenge for the title. Five years later in 1960 at Cherry Hills he was very much in the hunt, and only a flirtation with water on the 71st hole kept him out. This Championship marked the dawning of another era because the preceding four winners, Cary Middlecoff (1956), Dick Mayer (1957), Tommy Bolt (1958) and Billy Casper (1959) never captured the imagination in the same way as the 1960 champion.

Arnold Palmer did not do things by halves. His swashbuckling swing with the whiplash followthrough sometimes

Ken Venturi in the first Piccadilly Match-Play at Wentworth for which he had qualified as the 1964 US Open champion.

put the ball in no man's land but his powers of recovery were astonishing and this approach won the hearts of the nation. Starting that fateful last round at Cherry Hills, Palmer lay seven strokes off the pace but then proceded to birdie six of the first seven holes for an outward 30 and an eventual round of 65. It gave him victory by one stroke over a talented amateur named Jack Nicklaus. Over the next six years, Palmer challenged three more times for the title but each time lost a play-off. Gene Littler won in 1961 and then Nicklaus tied with Palmer at Oakmont in 1962 and the younger man won. In a rugged Championship at The Country Club in 1963, Palmer again tied, this time with Boros and Jackie Cupit, but lost to Boros, and in 1966 he suffered a crushing defeat at the hands of Billy Casper having led by seven strokes at Olympic with nine holes to play.

In between these traumas occurred one of the most emotional victories in the game as Ken Venturi finally won a major title that had so often been denied him. He had twice lost the Masters, once as an amateur in 1956 when he crumbled in the last round, and again in 1960 when Palmer birdied two of the final three holes to pip him. Wilting in the oppressive heat of Congressional,

Washington, Venturi fired a third-round 66 and then staggered to a 70 to win by four strokes.

The 1965 championship was held over the longest-ever course, Bellerive in Missouri, and it resulted in victory for perhaps the smallest of champions, Gary Player, who defeated Kel Nagle in a play-off. Player thus became the third man after Sarazen and Hogan to win all four of the Majors and he donated $25,000 from his prize of $26,000 to cancer research and the development of junior golf. Jack Nicklaus won at Baltusrol in 1967, firing a last round of 65 to beat Palmer by four strokes and lower the record aggregate to 275 as an unknown Mexican-American, Lee Trevino, finished fifth. He was not unknown after the next championship at Oak Hill where he became the first man to break 70 in all four rounds with a swing which made the purists shudder. Trevino's victory was followed by another shock winner in the shape of Orville Moody, a part-Indian who fired his arrows straight and true at Champions, Texas.

Tony Jacklin gave a tremendous fillip to British golf with his seven-stroke victory at Hazeltine in 1970. The course was extremely long and weather conditions poor but Jacklin thrived as his opponents complained about the course

Jack Nicklaus chats with former US Open champion Francis Ouimet before defending his title at The Country Club, Brookline in 1963.

with runner-up Dave Hill likening it to a cow pasture, a remark which cost him a heavy fine. Trevino defeated Nicklaus in a play-off at Merion in 1971 but the great man was not to be denied at Pebble Beach a year later when he took his third title in ten years. Johnny Miller's amazing last round of 63 in 1973 at Oakmont lowered the individual round record as he erupted from nowhere to win, but scoring at Winged Foot a year later was considerably higher and reflected the USGA's policy of letting the rough grow right up to the edges of the greens, Hale Irwin's aggregate winning score of 287 being seven over par. Lou Graham and John Mahaffey competed the 25th tie in the history of the US Open at Medinah in 1975, which Graham won, and in 1976 Mahaffey was again robbed of the title by Jerry Pate's magnificent 5-iron shot to the final hole of the Atlanta Country Club, Georgia, which finished a few feet from the hole.

Hubert Green won at Southern Hills, Oklahoma in 1977 playing the last few holes with an armed guard, following a telephoned threat on his life, and in 1978 Andy North bravely holed a putt of four feet on the last green at Cherry Hills to win. Hale Irwin captured his second title at Inverness in 1979 as prize money

rose to $300,000 and then it was the turn of that man again. All sorts of records fell to Jack Nicklaus at Baltusrol in 1980, including a Championship record-equalling 63 in the first round, the lowest 36-hole and 54-hole totals as well as a new record aggregate of 272. His four titles tied the records of Willie Anderson, Bobby Jones and Ben Hogan and the 18 years between his first and last victories

Tony Jacklin returns to England with the US Open trophy.

US Open specialist Andy North, winner in 1978 and 1985.

was the longest winning span.

The perfection of David Graham's winning last round of 67 at Merion in 1981 has never been matched: the Australian did not miss a fairway or a green in regulation figures, while in 1982 Tom Watson attained his own personal

David Graham on the final green at Merion in 1981.

state of Nirvana in winning at Pebble Beach by chipping in for a birdie at the 17th and birdieing the last hole to win by two strokes from Nicklaus. Watson was at his zenith and should have won at Oakmont in 1983. Play had been suspended overnight during the final round with four holes left for Watson and three for his closest challenger, Larry Nelson. Nelson resumed on the par-three 16th and put his tee shot 65 feet from the hole. Incredibly, with his second shot of the day, he holed the putt to give him the vital edge over Watson.

Moment of magic. Tom Watson dances with delight after sinking his chip on the 17th at Pebble Beach in 1982.

The carefree attitude of Fuzzy Zoeller belied a steely interior as he and Greg Norman fought out an epic duel at Winged Foot in 1984. Norman, playing just ahead of Zoeller, holed a monstrous putt on the final green which Zoeller, standing in the middle of the 18th fairway, thought was for a birdie three. In a memorable gesture, Zoeller waved a white towel in mock surrender but Norman's putt was only for a par four; moments later, Zoeller matched Norman's total and went on to win the play-off comfortably.

The amazing thing about Andy North's victory in 1985 at Oakland Hills was that it was only the third professional win of his career, two of which were US Opens. For some time it looked as though the title would be won by an Asian player, T.C. Chen, who led the field by four strokes going into the final round. Chen suffered the unusual penalty of hitting the ball twice while chipping from thick rough on the 5th hole in the final round and North stepped in.

The Championship returned to its roots in 1986 when it was staged at Shinnecock Hills, site of the second US Open in 1896. Rough and blustery weather swept the course which is the nearest to a links-type lay out in America, but Ray Floyd played cannily to win and bring his total of major titles to four (US Open, US Masters and two US PGA Championships). This left him on the threshold of being the fifth man to win all the Majors; he just needs the Open Championship to complete the set.

Prize-money for the US Open

Fuzzy Zoeller (left) and Greg Norman – play-off contestants in 1984 at Winged Foot.

now stands at over $700,000, and for an American player it represents the ultimate victory. The USGA has faced a constant barrage of criticism for setting up courses which are too tough, but this is unlikely to change for the aim is to examine every aspect of a player's game to the fullest extent. While there have been a few 'streaky' winners of the US Open, generally the race has gone to the most competent, and for a national Open that is how it should be.

The scoreboard behind Larry Nelson reflects his battle with Tom Watson over the final round in 1983.

US OPEN CHAMPIONSHIP

Year	Winner	Runner-up	Venue	By
1894	W Dunn (USA)	W Campbell (USA)	St Andrews, NY	2 holes

After 1894 decided by stroke play

Year	Winner	Country	Venue	Score
1895	H Rawlins	USA	Newport	173
1896	J Foulis	USA	Southampton	152
1897	J Lloyd	USA	Wheaton	162

72 holes played from 1898

Year	Winner	Country	Venue	Score
1898	F Herd	USA	Shinnecock Hills	328
1899	W Smith	USA	Baltimore	315
1900	H Vardon	GB	Wheaton	313
1901	W Anderson	USA	Myopia	315
1902	L Auchterlonie	USA	Garden City	305
1903	W Anderson	USA	Baltusrol	307
1904	W Anderson	USA	Glenview	304
1905	W Anderson	USA	Myopia	335
1906	A Smith	USA	Onwentsia	291
1907	A Ross	USA	Chestnut Hill	302
1908	F McLeod	USA	Myopia	322
1909	G Sargent	USA	Englewood	290
1910	A Smith	USA	Philadelphia	289
1911	J McDermott	USA	Wheaton	307
1912	J McDermott	USA	Buffalo	294
1913	F Ouimet (Am)	USA	Brookline	304
1914	W Hagen	USA	Midlothian	297
1915	J Travers (Am)	USA	Baltusrol	290
1916	C Evans (Am)	USA	Minneapolis	286
1919	W Hagen	USA	Braeburn	301
1920	E Ray	GB	Inverness	295
1921	J Barnes	USA	Washington	289
1922	G Sarazen	USA	Glencoe	288
1923	R Jones, jun (Am)	USA	Inwood	295
1924	C Walker	USA	Oakland Hills	297
1925	W MacFarlane	USA	Worcester	291
1926	R Jones, jun (Am)	USA	Scioto	293
1927	T Armour	USA	Oakmont	301
1928	J Farrell	USA	Olympic Fields	294
1929	R Jones, jun (Am)	USA	Winged Foot	294
1930	R Jones, jun (Am)	USA	Interlachen	287
1931	B Burke	USA	Inverness	292
1932	G Sarazen	USA	Fresh Meadow	286
1933	J Goodman (Am)	USA	North Shore	287
1934	O Dutra	USA	Merion	293
1935	S Parks	USA	Oakmont	299
1936	T Manero	USA	Springfield	282
1937	R Guldahl	USA	Oakland Hills	281
1938	R Guldahl	USA	Cherry Hills	284
1939	B Nelson	USA	Philadelphia	284
1940	W Lawson Little	USA	Canterbury	287
1941	C Wood	USA	Forth Worth	284
1946	L Mangrum	USA	Canterbury	284
1947	L Worsham	USA	St Louis	282
1948	B Hogan	USA	Los Angeles	276
1949	C Middlecoff	USA	Medinah	286
1950	B Hogan	USA	Merion	287
1951	B Hogan	USA	Oakland Hills	287
1952	J Boros	USA	Dallas	281
1953	B Hogan	USA	Oakmont	283
1954	E Furgol	USA	Baltusrol	284
1955	J Fleck	USA	San Francisco	287
1956	C Middlecoff	USA	Rochester	281
1957	R Mayer	USA	Inverness	282
1958	T Bolt	USA	Tulsa	283
1959	W Casper	USA	Winged Foot	282
1960	A Palmer	USA	Denver	280
1961	G Littler	USA	Birmingham	281
1962	J Nicklaus	USA	Oakmont	283
1963	J Boros	USA	Brookline	293

Year	Winner	Country	Venue	Score
1964	K Venturi	USA	Washington	278
1965	G Player	South Africa	St Louis	282
1966	W Casper	USA	San Francisco	278
1967	J Nicklaus	USA	Baltusrol	275
1968	L Trevino	USA	Rochester	275
1969	O Moody	USA	Houston	281
1970	A Jacklin	GB	Chaska	281
1971	L Trevino	USA	Merion	280
1972	J Nicklaus	USA	Pebble Beach	290
1973	J Miller	USA	Oakmont	279
1974	H Irwin	USA	Winged Foot	287
1975	L Graham	USA	Medinah	287
1976	J Pate	USA	Atlanta	277
1977	H Green	USA	Southern Hills	278
1978	A North	USA	Cherry Hills	285
1979	H Irwin	USA	Inverness	284
1980	J Nicklaus	USA	Baltusrol	272
1981	D Graham	Australia	Merion	273
1982	T Watson	USA	Pebble Beach	282
1983	L Nelson	USA	Oakmont	280
1984	F Zoeller	USA	Winged Foot	276
1985	A North	USA	Oakland Hills	279
1986	R Floyd	USA	Shinnecock Hills	279
1987	S Simpson	USA	San Francisco	277

The scoreboard tells the story of Andy North's win in 1985.

US PGA
CHAMPIONSHIP

The last of the four major championships
making up the modern Grand Slam, the
United States Professional Golfers'
Association Championship, is younger
than the Open Championship and the US
Open but older than the Masters. It was
first staged in 1916, the year the American
PGA was formed, which makes it the
second oldest tournament on the US Tour
behind the Western Open which began in
1899.

The PGA's standing in world golf
was certainly greater in the days when it
was a match-play event which made it
unique among the four championships.
The vagaries of match-play, which are in
fact its very essence, are not popular with
modern professionals who are weaned on
an exclusive diet of stroke-play, and the
demands of television have made the 18-
hole sprint an unsaleable item. Thus it
was in 1958 that the PGA succumbed to
these pressures and abandoned the match-
play format.

In its match-play years, the PGA
produced many exciting finishes and was
the perfect arena for the recovery skills of
Walter Hagen. He became the first
American-born winner in 1921 as Jim
Barnes (1916 and 1919) and Jock
Hutchison (1920) were both British-born
immigrants. Hagen was the supreme
match-player whose devastating ability to
roll three shots into two broke the hearts
of his opponents. His first victory was
followed by two in a row from Gene
Sarazen, the latter in 1923 coming after an
epic final with Hagen at Pelham, New
York which went to 38 holes but after that
Hagen was invincible for the next four
years. His run of 22 victorious matches
came to an end in 1928 when he was
defeated by the eventual winner, Leo
Diegel, in the third round. In typical
Hagen fashion, he said he had mislaid the
trophy in a taxi but it was eventually
recovered and Diegel put his name on it a
second time in 1929.

Tommy Armour, Tom Creavy and
Olin Dutra took the next three titles,
Dutra's year producing one of the most

Gene Sarazen (left) and
Walter Hagen (right) who
between them won the US
PGA from 1921-27 and
(centre) Tommy Armour
who beat Sarazen for the
title in 1930.

amazing turnarounds in the history of
championship golf when, in an early
round, Al Watrous stood nine up on
Bobby Cruickshank, all matches being
played over 36 holes. Watrous then
conceded a putt to Cruickshank which, if
missed, would have put Watrous 10 up
with 12 holes remaining. Cruickshank
started nibbling away at the lead and
squared the match with a long putt on the
36th green and then defeated poor
Watrous at the 41st.

Sarazen took his third title in
1933, and in 1934 Craig Wood lost to
Paul Runyan at the 38th. Sand-wedge
specialist Johnny Revolta won in 1935
and then Densmore Shute became the last

Densmore Shute, holder of
the US PGA title playing
in an invitation match
against Henry Cotton at
Walton Heath in 1937.

man to win two in a row. The 1938 final was billed as being no contest before the diminutive Runyan took on the power of Sam Snead. It turned out to be no contest the other way, as Runyan played a dazzling short game to demolish Snead by 8 and 7. Byron Nelson lost the 1939 final to Henry Picard but made amends the following year by defeating Snead 1 up. Nelson made five final appearances in the space of six stagings of the Championships, losing to Vic Ghezzi in the 1941 final, missing out in 1942 when Sam Snead won the first of his three PGAs, losing again in 1944 to Bob Hamilton and winning for a second time in 1945, the year he won 18 tournaments, 11 of them consecutively.

Ben Hogan took his first major title in 1946 with a typical destruction job on Ed Oliver by 6 and 4, and after Jim Ferrier won in 1947 Hogan was just as ruthless in 1948 when he beat Mike Turnesa by 7 and 6. Snead added two more in 1949 and 1951 with Chandler Harper intervening in 1950, but now the big names ceased to last through to the final and the Championship was poised to change to stroke-play. In 1953, for example, six former champions were beaten in the first two rounds and with Hogan absent through Open Championship duty at Carnoustie, the writing was on the wall. Lionel Hebert won the last match-play PGA in 1957, defeating Dow Finsterwald in the final, but by a strange quirk of fate Finsterwald came back the next year to win the first PGA at stroke-play. Victories by Bob Rosburg, Jay Hebert, brother of Lionel, and Jerry Barber followed and then came the first win by a foreigner, Gary Player in 1962.

Jack Nicklaus added his second major title of the year in 1963, having previously won the Masters, but the other member of the Big Three, Arnold Palmer, was to find that the PGA brought only that unwanted label of 'best player never to win it'. In 1964 Palmer broke 70 in every round at Columbus, Ohio but still had to give best to Bobby Nichols whose aggregate of 271 is still the record. Dave Marr had the effrontery to win in Palmer's

backyard of Laurel Valley, Pennsylvania in 1965 and he was followed by Al Geiberger in 1966 and Don January in 1967. At 48, Julius Boros became the oldest winner when he won at Pecan Valley, Texas in 1968 with Palmer second again, and then Ray Floyd won at Dayton, Ohio from Gary Player in an unpleasant atmosphere marred by anti-apartheid demonstrations against Player. In 1970 Palmer was second for the third time, to Dave Stockton at Southern Hills, and this Championship marked a return to US Open courses as venues.

The 1971 Chamiopship was held in February instead of its usual August date and it was marked by Jack Nicklaus's second win which gave him a second collection of the four major championships; a third was to follow, after his Open Championship victory at St Andrews in 1978. Gary Player won in 1972 at Oakland Hills, Michigan, another US Open course, and this win was highlighted by a 9-iron shot Player hit over trees and water to the 16th green which finished stone dead. The Nicklaus juggernaut continued to roll over the opposition and his third PGA title in 1973 enabled him to pass Bobby Jones's record of 13 Majors. Nicklaus was second to Lee Trevino in 1974 but was on top again in 1975, while Stockton repeated his win of 1970 with another in 1976, this time at Congressional, Washington.

The elegant swing and courageous spirit of Gene Littler, who had fought back from cancer, looked as though it would receive its just reward when he led by five strokes with nine holes to play at Pebble Beach in 1977 but a series of slips allowed Lanny Wadkins to catch him and it was Wadkins who won the play-off. Justice was done in 1978 at Oakmont when John Mahaffey tied with Jerry Pate and Tom Watson. Pate had snatched the US Open from Mahaffey in 1976 but this time it was Pate who could feel aggrieved as he missed a short putt on the 72nd green to fall into the tie and Mahaffey birdied the second extra hole to win.

Australia's David Graham became the second foreign winner after Player when he beat Ben Crenshaw in a

Al Geiberger, winner of the 1966 US PGA.

Above The unmistakable figures of Lee Trevino and Gary Player at Shoal Creek in 1984.

Right Bob Tway at his moment of victory in the 1986 US PGA.

play-off at Oakland Hills in 1979 and then Nicklaus again re-wrote the record books. His seven-stroke victory at Oak Hill in 1980 was the largest ever winning margin and he also equalled Hagen's record of five PGA titles. Larry Nelson won his first major title at the Atlanta Athletic Club, Georgia in 1981 and Ray Floyd took his second PGA at Southern Hills in 1982, his opening round of 63 tieing the lowest round in championship history. In only his second year as a professional, Hal Sutton, nick-named the 'Bear Apparent' because of his blond similarity to Nicklaus, held off Nicklaus himself at Riviera in 1983 for his first major championship. The evergreen Lee

Trevino kept out another ageless wonder, Gary Player, in winning at Shoal Creek, Alabama in 1984, ten years after his first PGA victory, and then Trevino challenged again in 1985 at Cherry Hills but had to give best to Hubert Green.

The 1986 Championship at Inverness found Greg Norman in his usual place at the head of the field after three rounds, this time four strokes ahead of Bob Tway with a round to go. Norman was still four ahead with nine to play but Tway drew level and at the final hole dramatically holed out from a greenside bunker for a birdie which Norman couldn't match.

US PGA CHAMPIONSHIP

Year	Winner	Runner-up	Venue	By
1916	J Barnes	J Hutchison	Siwanoy	1 hole
1919	J Barnes	F McLeod	Engineers' Club	6 and 5
1920	J Hutchison	D Edgar	Flossmoor	1 hole
1921	W Hagen	J Barnes	Inwood Club	3 and 2
1922	G Sarazen	E French	Oakmont	4 and 3
1923	G Sarazen	W Hagen	Pelham	38th hole
1924	W Hagen	J Barnes	French Lick	2 holes
1925	W Hagen	WE Mehlhorn	Olympic Fields	6 and 4
1926	W Hagen	L Diegel	Salisbury	4 and 3
1927	W Hagen	J Turnesa	Dallas	1 hole
1928	L Diegel	A Espinosa	Five Farms	6 and 5
1929	L Diegel	J Farrell	Hill Crest	6 and 4
1930	T Armour	G Sarazen	Fresh Meadow	1 hole
1931	T Creavy	D Shute	Wannamoisett	2 and 1
1932	O Dutra	F Walsh	St Paul	4 and 3
1933	G Sarazen	W Goggin	Milwaukee	5 and 4
1934	P Runyan	C Wood	Buffalo	38th hole
1935	J Revolta	T Armour	Oklahoma	5 and 4
1936	D Shute	J Thomson	Pinehurst	3 and 2
1937	D Shute	H McSpaden	Pittsburgh	37th hole
1938	P Runyan	S Snead	Shawnee	8 and 7
1939	H Picard	B Nelson	Pomonok	3 th hole
1940	B Nelson	S Snead	Hershey	1 hole
1941	V Ghezzie	B Nelson	Denver	38th hole
1942	S Snead	J Turnesa	Atlantic City	2 and 1
1943	*No Championship*			
1944	R Hamilton	B Nelson	Spokane	1 hole
1945	B Nelson	S Byrd	Dayton	4 and 3
1946	B Hogan	E Oliver	Portland	6 and 4
1947	J Ferrier	C Harbert	Detroit	2 and 1
1948	B Hogan	M Turnesa	Norwood Hills	7 and 6
1949	S Snead	J Palmer	Richmond	3 and 2
1950	C Harper	H Williams	Scioto	4 and 3
1951	S Snead	W Burkemo	Oakmont	7 and 6
1952	J Turnesa	C Harbert	Big Spring, Louisville	1 hole
1953	W Burkemo	F Lorza	Birmingham	2 and 1
1954	C Herbert	W Burkemo	St Paul	4 and 3
1955	D Ford	C Middlecoff	Detroit	4 and 3
1956	J Burke	T Kroll	Boston	3 and 2
1957	L Hebert	D Finsterwald	Miami Valley	3 and 1

After 1957 decided by stroke play

Year	Winner	Score	Venue	Year	Winner	Score	Venue
1958	D Finsterwald	276	Llanerch	1973	J Nicklaus	277	Canterbury
1959	B Rosburg	277	Minneapolis	1974	L Trevino	276	Tanglewood
1960	J Hebert	281	Firestone	1975	J Nicklaus	276	Firestone
1961	J Barber	277	Olympic Fields	1976	D Stockton	281	Congressional
1962	G Player	278	Aronomink	1977	L Wadkins	287	Pebble Beach
1963	J Nicklaus	279	Dallas	1978	J Mahaffey	276	Oakmont
1964	B Nichols	271	Columbus	1979	D Graham	272	Oakland Hills
1965	D Marr	280	Laurel Valley	1980	J Nicklaus	274	Oak Hill
1966	A Geiberger	280	Firestone	1981	L Nelson	273	Atlanta
1967	D January	281	Columbine	1982	R Floyd	272	Southern Hills
1968	J Boros	281	Pecan Valley	1983	H Sutton	274	Riviera
1969	R Floyd	276	Dayton	1984	L Trevino	273	Shoal Creek
1970	D Stockton	279	Southern Hills	1985	H Green	278	Cherry Hills
1971	J Nicklaus	281	PGA National	1986	R Tway	276	Inverness
1972	G Player	281	Oakland Hills	1987	L Nelson	287	West Palm Beach

WORLD MATCH-PLAY

'Match-play's the thing,' said Freddie Tait, British Amateur champion in 1896 and 1898, 'stroke-play's so much rifle-shooting.' Most amateur golfers will understand Tait's sentiments since match-play is the form of golf which is most popular at their level. On the other hand, professional golfers spend the greatest part of their careers engaged in the rifle-shooting of stroke-play and regard match-play with the highest suspicion. The fact that a player can go round in 68 and lose while another can produce a 75 and win is unacceptable to the modern money-making machines while the awful abruptness of a match-play defeat leaves no room for excuses.

Fortunately for golf and the professional game in particular, there is one match-play event which has resisted the stroke-play trend and stands as one of the classic championships of the world. The World Match-Play Championship, now under the aegis of Suntory but still often referred to by long-term devotees as the Piccadilly has, since its inception in 1964, created an atmosphere which puts it on the fringe of major championship status. Maybe the taint of commercial sponsorship has prevented it from being acknowledged as the fifth Major, but just as April means the Masters and July the Open Championship, so it is that October means the Match-Play at Wentworth. The permanency of the venue is an integral part of the tournament's success but it is the history of blood-and-guts encounters which have sustained its appeal.

The original concept was to bring together the eight best players of the year and pit them against one another over 36 holes. The field for that first Championship contained the charismatic figure of Arnold Palmer, the current US Masters champion, Tony Lema, the Open champion, Gary Player, Jack Nicklaus, Ken Venturi, the US Open champion, and Bruce Devlin, with Peter Butler and Neil Coles providing the British interest. The event was given a rousing start when Palmer beat off the stubborn resistance of Coles in the final, eventually holing a birdie putt on the 35th green to win by 2 and 1.

Just as Gene Sarazen launched the US Masters in its second staging with his albatross two on the 15th, so the semi-final match of 1965 between Gary Player and Tony Lema put the Match-Play in the forefront of golfing legend. The events of that match have virtually been carved in tablets of stone and it is enough to say that there has never been a match like it. In the morning round Lema cruised round in an effortless 67 to lunch six up. He went seven up at the first hole of the afternoon and that, to all intents and purposes, was that, As the crowd drifted away, only one man believed that there was any hope and Gary Player began to put that belief into practice. He was still five down with nine holes left but only three down with seven remaining. He was two down after 13 and then only one down with two to play. Player holed a nasty putt of five feet on the 35th hole to stay in the match and then on the 18th, after Lema had hooked his second shot to this par five in the classic reflex action of a man in acute distress, Player hit the shot that seemed to be guided by some unseen hand. Launching himself into his second shot with a 4-wood, Player sent the ball perilously close to the trees on the right but it travelled through the branches unscathed and rolled up onto the green to within ten feet of the hole for a winning birdie. Lema was completely shattered and had no answer to Player's solid par four at the 37th. Victory over Peter Thomson in the final was something of an anti-climax but it gave the South African the first of five victories in the event, the last coming in 1973 in another cliff-hanger when he defeated Graham Marsh at the 40th hole of the final.

Player successfully defended the title in 1966, defeating Arnold Palmer in the semi-finals and Jack Nicklaus in the final. This was the match which included the famous sign-board incident on the 9th hole when Nicklaus was refused relief from an advertising hoarding on his line by the referee, Tony Duncan. There was no relief either for Nicklaus from Player's onslaught and the little man outgunned

Above Jack Nicklaus, who was to have problems with rulings in subsequent World Match-Play events, discusses his position during the 1964 competition with opponent Bruce Devlin.

Top Arnold Palmer shakes hands with Neil Coles after winning the first World Match-Play title in 1964.

his opponent by 6 and 4. It was Palmer's turn again in 1967 when he had the satisfaction of beating Peter Thomson on the final green. This match engendered mutual respect between the two with Thomson conceding that he was beaten by the better man.

The Player/Palmer monopoly continued in 1968 with Player gaining his third final victory, over Bob Charles by one hole. Charles was not to be denied in 1969 when, with a magical display of putting, he beat Gene Littler on the 37th hole of the final, having holed from 25 feet on the final green to save the match.

Nicklaus finally captured the title in 1970 after a splendid final with Lee Trevino and then reached the final again in 1971 where he faced his old rival, Player. Nicklaus was one up at lunch but there was no holding Player in the afternoon and he romped home by 5 and 4.

The following year is remembered not so much for Tom Weiskopf's victory over Trevino but more for the magnificent semi-final between Trevino and Tony Jacklin. Having suffered cruelly at the hands of the American in that year's Open Championship at Muirfield, Jacklin was determined not to let Trevino's constant chatter get to him and made his intentions plain by saying he

was not going to talk. 'You don't have to talk, Tony,' said Trevino, 'just listen.'

After the morning round, Jacklin was listening to a four-hole deficit but he came out in the afternoon like a lion. He quelled Trevino's ebullience with an outward 29 but still the American kept his nose in front and finally sealed victory with a beautifully fashioned second shot to the final green which made Jacklin's round of 63 a statistical irrelevance.

Player received his comeuppance in 1974 when he lost his first final at the accomplished hands of Hale Irwin who proved how tough he was by winning

again in 1975 and reaching the final in 1976. This time toughness was no match for the man with a golden putter and David Graham's recovery over the last nine holes left spectators open-mouthed in disbelief and, less surprisingly, Irwin wasn't too impressed either. Putt after putt from Graham dived into the hole except one on the 35th which just toppled in to keep the Australian in the match, after which there was no question who would hole on the 37th green for the title.

That was the last year of Piccadilly's sponsorship and the tournament was taken over by the vast Colgate conglomerate with the field being expanded to 16 players and seedings introduced. It was an unhappy transition as the next two years produced little that was memorable in terms of drama but did see Marsh extract some revenge for 1973 with a well-deserved victory in 1977, and Isao Aoki became the first Japanese victor the following year.

Above Isao Aoki and Bill Rogers discuss the priorities after matching drives during the 1979 final.

Left Five-times winner Gary Player is congratulated by Jack Nicklaus after his fourth win in 1971.

During Suntory's stewardship the Championship has recaptured some of its former glory with the first four Suntory finals going to the 36th hole or beyond. Bill Rogers remains the only American winner in an eight-year spell when, with a magnificent pitch to the last green, he defeated Aoki in 1979, but since then the title has been the exclusive property of two men, Severiano Ballesteros and Greg Norman. Norman beat Sandy Lyle in 1980 by one hole, and Ballesteros beat Ben Crenshaw in 1981 by one hole and then repeated the trick by holing a monstrous putt across the 37th green to oust the unfortunate Lyle. It was Norman's turn again in 1983 when he beat Nick Faldo in the final by 3 and 2. This was the year of the unfortunate incident when, in an earlier round, Faldo was playing Graham Marsh and struck his second shot through the back of the 16th green. After a lapse of several seconds, the ball reappeared from the crowd onto the green and, since it was then decided that the ball had not come to rest but had been deflected while still in motion, Faldo was allowed to play it where it finished.

Ballesteros took his total of victories to four over the next two years by

Left Greg Norman with Nick Faldo during the World Match-Play final of 1983.

Below Bernhard Langer at the 14th during the first of two successive finals which he was to lose to Seve Ballesteros.

beating Bernhard Langer in the finals of 1984 and 1985, and although Lyle made his third appearance in a final again in 1986, he succumbed to Norman. This Championship marked the return to Wentworth of Jack Nicklaus after a prolonged absence. He dealt with the precocious talents of Jose-Maria Olazabal in his first match but lost an absorbing semi-final to Greg Norman by one hole. All paled however, in the light of the second-round match between Lyle and Japan's Tsuneyuki Nakajima in which both players produced rounds of 65 and 64 to set a new scoring record for the event; Lyle eventually won this match, which neither really deserved to lose, at the 38th.

So the tradition of stirring encounters has been maintained with superlative golf from one player sparking off a similar response from his opponent. By comparison, the weekly stroke-play grind is tame stuff. Indeed, match-play's the thing and the World Match-Play is the best thing about it.

A barrage of birdies for Sandy Lyle and 'Tommy' Nakajima during their semi-final in 1986.

WORLD MATCH PLAY CHAMPIONSHIP

Sponsored by Piccadilly until 1976; by Colgate 1977 and 1978; and by Suntory from 1979 and played each year at Wentworth

Year	Winner	Runner-up	By
1964	A Palmer (USA)	N Coles (GB)	2 and 1
1965	G Player (South Africa)	P Thomson (Australia)	3 and 2
1966	G Player (South Africa)	J Nicklaus (USA)	6 and 4
1967	A Palmer (USA)	P Thomson (Australia)	1 hole
1968	G Player (South Africa)	R Charles (New Zealand)	1 hole
1969	R Charles (New Zealand)	G Littler (USA)	37th hole
1970	J Nicklaus (USA)	L Trevino (USA)	2 and 1
1971	G Player (South Africa)	J Nicklaus (USA)	5 and 4
1972	T Weiskopf (USA)	L Trevino (USA)	4 and 3
1973	G Player (South Africa)	G Marsh (Australia)	40th hole
1974	H Irwin (USA)	G Player (South Africa)	3 and 1
1975	H Irwin (USA)	A Geiberger (USA)	4 and 2
1976	D Graham (Australia)	H Irwin (USA)	38th hole
1977	G Marsh (Australia)	R Floyd (USA)	5 and 3
1978	I Aoki (Japan)	S Owen (New Zealand)	3 and 2
1979	W Rogers (USA)	I Aoki (Japan)	1 hole
1980	G Norman (Australia)	S Lyle (GB)	1 hole
1981	S Ballesteros (Spain)	B Crenshaw (USA)	1 hole
1982	S Ballesteros (Spain)	S Lyle (GB)	37th hole
1983	G Norman (Australia)	N Faldo (GB)	3 and 2
1984	S Ballesteros (Spain)	B Langer (West Germany)	2 and 1
1985	S Ballesteros (Spain)	B Langer (West Germany)	6 and 5
1986	G Norman (Australia)	S Lyle (GB)	2 and 1

GREAT ADVICE

Golfers are constantly besieged by advice. Some of it comes from well-meaning friends, some is gleaned from books and magazines – and there are actually golfers who take the trouble to have a lesson from a professional!

There is really no substitute for a lesson under the watchful eye of someone who knows what he is talking about and in whom you have confidence. Most golfers, however, prefer to spend time actually playing rather than taking a lesson, and so they learn to play with what they have rather than by trying to improve their method. This chapter is designed to provide advice which can be easily assimilated into anybody's game without any radical adjustments and it contains many of the key thoughts of some of the world's greatest players. What they have to say about the varied aspects of the game can only help you with yours.

PACE YOUR STANCE

Golfers who are confused about how far apart to set their feet when they stand to the ball can use this handy piece of information expounded by Ben Crenshaw. Simply take a few steps and then stop with your feet a pace apart. Maintaining this position, turn and face towards an imaginary ball. This will provide a natural width to your stance.

HOLD THE BIRD

When it comes to holding the golf club, the word 'grip' is something of a misnomer. Grip implies strength and rigidity, and if you grip the club too strongly the tension in your forearms will reduce clubhead speed through the ball. Also, remember that a tight grip can only loosen during the swing, while a light grip will firm up at impact. In finding the correct grip pressure, Johnny Miller uses the analogy of imagining you are holding a small bird in your hands: you don't want the bird to escape but you don't want to crush it. A light grip promotes release of the clubhead through the ball.

INITIATING THE SWING

In moving-ball games, the way the ball approaches the player triggers off a reflex action for the hitting. Since golf is played to a stationary ball, the player has to initiate the action himself from a static position. If the start of the swing is made from a completely static position then the swing itself is likely to be jerky and lacking in a smooth tempo. All great players use some form of 'forward press' to initiate the backswing. Gary Player has a very noticeable forward press whereby he kicks in his right knee prior to the start of the swing whereas Jack Nicklaus turns his head slightly to the right just before he takes the club back. These movements help to break down any rigidity that may occur in addressing the ball.

PICKING THE SPOT

Golf is a target game but it is extremely difficult to line yourself up on a target 200 yards away. It is much easier to line up the clubhead on a target a few feet away from you. When you see the top professionals stand behind the ball before addressing it, they are picking a spot in line with the ball and the target. It may be a leaf or a blade of grass, but they use it to make sure the face of the club is pointing at the target.

RAISE THE CLUB TO RELIEVE TENSION

In addressing the ball, many golfers press

the club into the ground quite firmly. This promotes tension through the forearms and usually results in a violent and unsuccessful attack on the ball. If you watch Sam Torrance or Jack Nicklaus closely you will note that in addressing the ball, they keep the clubhead a few inches off the ground. This helps them to make a free and easy start to the swing and has the added bonus of not subjecting them to any penalty should the ball move while they are addressing it.

DEVELOP A STOCK SHOT

One of the reasons why Lee Trevino has been so successful in his career is that his standard shot is a fade. Even in moments of intense pressure, Trevino knows how the ball is going to behave on each shot. If you want to be able to perform under pressure, then it is sensible to try and develop a stock shot, one that will keep the ball in the fairway. It may be a drawn shot or a faded shot but if you can produce it then your chances of finishing among the winners will be greatly increased.

BLAST FROM THE PATH

Very often, shots that miss the green finish up on one of the well-worn paths round the side of the green or, worse, end up in a divot mark. These shots create panic, particularly if there is a bunker between the ball and the hole. The solution is to play the ball like a bunker shot. Play the ball back towards the right foot and open your stance. Use a sand wedge and hit down hard about an inch behind the ball – if the shot is 20 yards, use enough force to hit the ball 40 yards. The ball will fly up high and land very softly with left to right spin. Severiano Ballesteros is a master of this shot, and with a little practice you can make it an effective shot in your repertoire.

TOE THE FAST PUTT

This is a putting tip used by Greg Norman and many other top players. When you face a downhill putt on a fast green, address the ball off the toe of the putter and try and hit the ball with the toe. Because this part of the putter-face is away from the sweet spot in the centre, it will have the effect of deadening the speed of the ball off the face. The result is that the ball starts its journey at a slower pace which is what you want on putts of this nature.

PUTT THROUGH THE TEES

This putting exercise, devised by 1964 US Open champion Ken Venturi, can help to build your confidence on the greens. For short putts, place two tees on either side of the hole and concentrate on rolling the ball between the two tees. On long putts, determine the break and then put two tees ahead of you at the point where the break begins. Then roll the ball through the tees at the right pace. This exercise will help you to build a smooth stroke.

FIND THE BALL

Golfers who consistently hit the ball off the heel or the toe of the club could benefit from this practice exercise that is a particular favourite of Henry Cotton. Walk down the fairway and knock a ball along with just the right hand. Then stop and hit the ball with both hands and you'll find you'll hit the ball in the middle of the clubface because your right hand now knows where the ball is. Repeat this drill with the left hand. Cotton is also famous for his advocacy of hitting a car tyre in order to build up strength in the hands. Hit the tyre with either hand and then with the hands together.

TIE UP YOUR STROKE

Any kind of body movement during the putting stroke is usually destructive but it is also hard to detect. To check if your body is moving, wear a tie the next time you practise. As you stand over the ball, the tie will hang down and any movement will cause the tie to wave around. You won't be able to keep the tie completely still but you'll become more aware of staying still over the ball.

USE A HANDKERCHIEF IN THE RAIN

In persistent rain, the main things to keep dry are your grips. If, however, your grips become too wet to hold properly, you could benefit from this little trick that Tom Watson uses. Simply wrap a dry handkerchief around the grip when you hold the club. The Rules allow this and it will maintain your grip on the club without any loss of feel.

STAY IN THE PRESENT

Successful golf is very often a state of mind, but as success builds up during a round it is all too easy to let the mind wander ahead. Tony Jacklin used to make a point of concentrating on the shot he was about to play rather than one he might have to play a few holes later. Staying in the present allows you to direct your physical and mental energies to the shot facing you rather than one in the future.

GRIP FIRMLY IN LONG GRASS

If you face a chip or pitch from very long grass then follow the advice of Lee Trevino. He believes in gripping the club tightly to prevent it turning as it moves through the thick stuff. The shot is played with no wrist movement and at a rhythmic pace with the clubhead leading the hands through the ball.

USE THE CLOCK FOR CORRECT CLUBHEAD PATH

The correct mental image of the way the clubhead should approach the ball can be achieved by picturing a clock-face. Imagine the ball is at the centre of the clock and then see the clubhead entering the clock-face at 4 o'clock and, passing through the ball, leaving the clock-face at 10 o'clock. Tony Jacklin recommends this as one of the best ways of curing an out-to-in clubhead path.

KEEP THE BALL DOWN WITH MORE CLUB

It is usually recommended that if you want to hit a low 'knockdown' shot you should position the ball back in your stance and move your hands ahead of the ball. Fuzzy Zoeller, winner of the 1979 US Masters and 1984 US Open, thinks those instructions are too complex for the average player. He believes in keeping it simple and says if you want to hit a 'knockdown' shot, just take two clubs more than the shot requires, say a 7-iron instead of a 9-iron and hit the shot easier. The loft of the club will keep the ball down and because you don't hit down on the ball so hard, it will fly lower.

PITCH INTO THE UMBRELLA

Your golf umbrella can become a useful practice aid in your own garden when you want to sharpen up your pitching. Simply use an open, upturned umbrella as your target and gently loft balls into it using a sand-wedge. Tee the ball up on a tuft to prevent damage to the grass. Practising to a specific target in this manner will help develop feel and control.

MAKE YOUR OPPONENT WIN THE HOLE

Graham Marsh, winner of the 1977 World Match-Play Championship, has one golden rule for match-play golf – always make your opponent win the hole. For example, if your opponent is on the green in two and you are short in two, try and get your chip as close as possible so that he thinks he has to hole his putt to win. It's surprising the number of times a player three putts when he thinks he has to hole a putt to win. Never hand your opponent a hole by giving up in a seemingly hopeless situation.

GIVE AN INCH FOR BETTER PUTTER ALIGNMENT

Many putts are missed because the putter is incorrectly lined up to the hole. To help putter alignment, place the blade about an inch behind the ball instead of right up against it. Your eyes can then more easily see if the putter is aimed along the intended path. When you are confident that the putter is aimed correctly, you can move it in close to the ball.

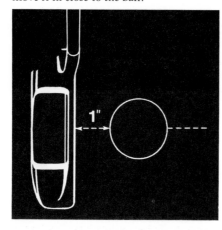

EVERY PUTT IS STRAIGHT

Bobby Locke, generally acknowledged as one of the finest putters the game has ever seen, had a simple philosophy on the greens. Early in his career he established a set routine before each putt which never varied. He used it to fix the idea in his mind that every putt was straight, it was only the fall of the ground which made the ball swing. Using this thought can help clear your mind of thinking too much about allowing for the borrow. Locke also made a meticulous study of the area around the hole itself, for if the grass was worn away on one side of the hole on a breaking putt, this showed which side of the hole the ball was most likely to go.

GRIP THICKNESS CAN HELP YOU

If you slice the ball, then a change in grip thickness could help. A lack of wrist action often contributes to a slice, so a change to thinner grips on your clubs will mean the grip is more in the fingers and a more lively wrist action will result. Conversely, if you hook the ball a change to thicker grips will reduce wrist action by placing the grip more in the palms of the hands.

A PUTT IS BETTER THAN A CHIP

Arnold Palmer has always maintained that your worst putt will be as good as your best chip when you are faced with a shot from the fringe of the green with nothing in the way. Provided the grass is smooth and the grain is running away from you, it is always more advisable to putt the ball rather than chip it. On a shot of 50 feet, you would have to hit a pretty good chip to get the ball within five feet of the hole, but even a moderate putt should get the ball within the same range.

CHECK YOUR GRIP WITH A BLADE OF GRASS

If you are constantly hitting behind the ball and/or hooking, it is likely that the hands are separating at the top of the swing. To check if this is happening, John Jacobs recommends placing a blade of grass on top of the left thumb and, with the right palm in place, practise hitting the ball without dislodging the grass. Players such as Gary Player have been helped by this suggestion.

ACCELERATE THE HANDLE OF THE PUTTER

Inconsistent putting is usually the result of the putterhead decelerating at impact, particularly on short putts. To make sure you accelerate the putter through the ball, think of moving the handle of the club past the left knee. This will ensure a solid contact and provide more consistency.

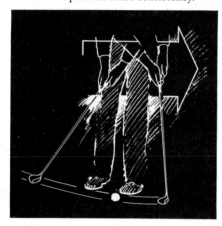

COUNT YOUR SWING PACE

Most golfers swing the club too fast on the backswing which makes it difficult to build momentum on the downswing. Pacing your swing provides an even tempo which creates power. Tom Watson advises that any golfer can improve tempo by simply counting 'one' on the backswing and 'two' on the downswing. When you first try this on the practice ground you will probably find that you are hitting the ball at 'one and a half'. This means your tempo is too fast so concentrate on making the hit at 'two'.

LEARN FROM YOUR TEE PEG

If you are constantly breaking tees or knocking them out of the ground when using your driver, it means that your angle of approach is too steep and the clubhead is travelling too much towards the ground. To encourage a more sweeping contact, tee up a ball and place the driver behind it. Then swing the club over the ball three or four times without making contact. Then rest the club behind the ball and try and hit the ball without touching the tee. Severiano

Ballesteros can hit ten successive drives without disturbing the tee, proof that his angle of approach is correct.

USE A TEE ON THE SHORT HOLES

Tom Watson believes that too many golfers think it is a sign of strength to throw the ball down on the grass for a tee shot on a short hole. If you do this, you have no idea how the ball is going to react off the clubface at impact. Teeing the ball up with all of the stem of the tee in the ground means you get a consistent reaction from the ball off the clubface.

PUTT ALONGSIDE THE WALL

You can groove a repeating putting stroke by practising indoors against a wall. Place the ball close to the wall with the toe of the putter just touching the skirting board. If you take the putter back on the correct path, you will notice it will gradually move away from the skirting board. The renowned British teacher John Jacobs recommends this exercise to develop the correct path of the putter through the stroke.

CURE THE SHANK

The most common cause of a shank is a backswing that is too flat. Sam Snead provides this simple remedy for golf's most destructive shot by asking his pupils to concentrate on pointing the club shaft towards the sky on the backswing. This eradicates the flat backswing and stops the shank.

MATCH YOUR SHOULDERS TO THE SLOPE

A ball lying on the upslope of a bunker looks inviting to hit but very often the shot is unsuccessful. This is because the golfer digs his feet into the sand and keeps his shoulders level. Expert bunker player Ray Floyd reveals that this is why the club buries well behind the ball and the shot fails. To correct this, set up so that your shoulders are parallel with the slope with most of the body weight on the right foot. Your swing will then follow the slope and you can play the shot taking the normal amount of sand.

THE STORY OF WOMEN'S GOLF

As far as is known, the first reference to women playing golf was made at Musselburgh in 1810 when the minutes of a meeting held on 10 December contained this item: 'The Club resolve to present by subscription a new Creel and Shawl to the best female golfer who plays on the annual occasion on 1st Jan. next, old style (12th Jan. new) to be intimated to the Fish Ladies by the Officer of the Club. Two of the best Barcelona silk handkerchiefs to be added to the above premium of the Creel.'

On the other hand, it is well recorded that at the trial of Mary Queen of Scots in 1584, the prosecution made great play of the fact that, a few days after the death of her husband, Lord Darnley, she was seen playing golf in the fields beside Seton.

Leading ladies and their caddies after the Ladies' Golf Championship of 1895 at Portrush. (Left to right) Lady Margaret Scott (the winner), Miss E. Lithgoe, Miss H.C. Willock and Mrs Ryder Richardson.

Neither of these dates is imperishably enshrined in the annals of the game as being when golf really caught on among the ladies. Progress was slow and even when in 1868 the Westward Ho! and North Devon Ladies Club was formed, the first of its kind, play was restricted to between May and October and only with a putter at that. The Victorian age being well entrenched, vigorous exercise for ladies was discouraged and the mode of dress at that time made a full swing impossible. But changes were on the way and other ladies' Clubs came into being such as the London Scottish Ladies, formed in 1872, who played over Wimbledon Common and later became Wimbledon Ladies. It was from this club that Miss Issette Pearson went forth and formed the Ladies' Golf Union (LGU) in 1893, the governing body of the ladies' game, amid much male scepticism that the women were physically unsuited for golf and were bound to fall out and quarrel. Despite this attitude, which still prevails at some clubs today, the women also started, in 1893, the British Women's Amateur Championship held over the ladies' links of the Lytham and St Annes Club.

The first Championship was won by Lady Margaret Scott with ridiculous ease. She had a course round her father's house (he being Lord Eldon) and played constantly with her three brothers, all of them scratch players and one of whom, the Hon. Michael Scott, went on to win the Amateur Championship in 1933. Lady Margaret won the title for the next two years and then retired from competitive golf.

In 1897 the Championship was staged in Scotland for the first time, at Gullane, and was dominated by the three Orr sisters of North Berwick, two of whom met in the final. Lottie Dod, who won in 1904, had previously won the women's singles at Wimbledon on five occasions. Despite her versatility, however, the standard of women's golf did not significantly improve until 1908, when it was suddenly uplifted by one player. She was Cecil Leitch, one of five golfing sisters from Silloth, and she brought a new dimension to the women's game which hitherto had been lacking. Exhibiting a wide stance and a strong grip, Miss Leitch gave the ball an uncompromising hit, her iron play being particularly forceful. She did not win the title until 1914, and then after the war she returned to win it again in 1920 and 1921. By then she had a serious and deadly rival at her heels in Joyce Wethered, sister of Roger Wethered who had lost the play-off for the 1921 Open Championship.

The two met in the final of the British Women's Championship and Miss Leitch was victorious, but they had also met in the final of the 1920 English Women's Championship at Sheringham and on that occasion Miss Wethered had won, the first of five consecutive victories in that event. They met twice more in the final of the British Women's in 1922 and 1925 with Miss Wethered winning on

both occasions, in 1925 at Troon after a classic match which went to the 37th. For the next three years Miss Wethered did not play in the Championship and Miss Leitch added a fourth victory to her list. In 1929 the event was staged at St Andrews, which prompted Miss Wethered to enter and she duly progressed to the final where she faced Miss Glenna Collett, the outstanding American player of that time. In what is generally regarded as the finest final in the history of the event, Miss Wethered fought back from five down early in the morning round to two down at lunch and then played the first nine holes of the afternoon round in 35 strokes to go four up, eventually winning by 3 and 1.

That was Joyce Wethered's last

appearance in the Championship, but her influence on the women's game remains to this day. In an era when Hagen, Sarazen and Jones were permanently in the limelight, her achievements did not perhaps receive the recognition they deserved. Her simple swing and incisive striking, based on rhythm and timing, caused Bobby Jones to comment that he felt she was the finest striker of a ball, man or woman, he had ever seen. Her powers of concentration have also passed into the folklore of the game, exemplified by her famous comment 'What train?' when she holed a putt during the final of the English Championship as an express roared past.

Meanwhile, the women's game was also well established in America. The

Above Joyce Wethered at the Ladies' Championship, 1925.

Left Cecil Leitch in 1908, at the beginning of an outstanding career.

Margaret Curtis, who with her sister Harriot donated the Curtis Cup.

US Women's Amateur Championship began in 1895 and in 1896 produced its first teenage champion in 16-year-old Beatrix Hoyt, who completed a hat-trick of wins and then, like Lady Margaret Scott, retired from the scene. The Curtis sisters, Harriot and Margaret, donors of the Curtis Cup (see below), achieved a unique distinction when both reached the final in 1907, Margaret winning the first of her three titles. Then Alexa Stirling, who had been taught by Bobby Jones's mentor, Stewart Maiden, emerged to win three titles in a row, in 1916 and, after a break for the war, 1919 and 1920. From 1922 to 1935, the title was won six times by Glenna Collett and three times by Virginia van Wie. In 1936 a British player, Pam Barton, did what no other British lady golfer has done since. She won the title, and she also won the British Women's in the same year. Pam Barton was an exuberant golfer with a fearless approach and would certainly have had more influence on the game if she had not been killed in a flying accident during World War II.

Following a visit to Britain in 1905, the Curtis sisters developed a desire to bring the lady golfers of both nations together in a spirit of friendly rivalry. Thus the Curtis Cup was born and first staged at Wentworth in 1932. Like its counterparts in the men's game, the Ryder and Walker Cups, the Curtis Cup has been dominated by the Americans. It is contested every two years on a home and away basis, and until 1986 Britain had achieved two ties, in 1936 at Gleneagles and in 1958 at Brae Burn, Massachusetts, and two victories, in 1952 at Muirfield and in 1956 at Prince's. The 1986 match, however, saw a milestone passed when the British won for the first time on American soil, defeating the home side convincingly at Prairie Dunes, Kansas.

The next great figure to appear on the scene was Mildrid Didrikson Zaharias, known universally as 'The Babe'. She was born in 1914, the youngest of seven children, and she developed into quite the most extraordinary woman athlete of all time. Before she turned to golf she entered three events at the 1932

Above The multi-talented 'Babe' Zaharias.

Left Mrs E.H. Vare (formerly Glenna Collett), the American captain and reigning US Ladies' champion, drives off during the tied Curtis Cup match of 1936 at Gleneagles.

Olympics, the low hurdles, the javelin and the high jump. She won all three, but was prevented from receiving the gold medal in the high jump because her style was illegal. With no athletic fields left to conquer she took up golf and quickly showed her mastery of that game as well.

In 1935 she won the Texas Open and, after taking some prize-money, lost her amateur status. She was reinstated in 1943 and won the US Amateur in 1946, and took Britain by storm in 1947, winning the British Women's title. She then reverted to being a professional and won the US Women's Open in 1948, 1950 and 1954, the latter victory coming after she had undergone surgery for cancer, the disease finally claiming her life in 1956. 'The Babe' drove the ball prodigious distances even though she was not heavily built or particularly tall. Her swing was lithesome and she attacked the ball tigerishly. When asked the secret of her great length, she uttered the immortal phrase: 'I just loosen my girdle and belt it.'

The inauguration of the US Open in 1946 was largely due to 'The Babe' and another outstanding amateur, Patty Berg. In the same year, the Women's Professional Golfers' Association was formed, a short-lived union which was replaced in 1950 by the Ladies' Professional Golfers' Association. This was the brain-child of Fred Corcoran, a former executive director of the Men's Tour, who believed there was a place for women's professional golf and set about raising $45,000 for nine tournaments. Most of this went to Mrs Zaharias and Miss Berg who between them won 19 out of 23 events in the first two years. Compared with the Men's Tour, growth in prize-money was slow and although players such as Mickey Wright, Betsy Rawls and Carol Mann showed they could produce low scores – Miss Wright firing a 62 in a tournament in 1964 – they had a struggle to capture the imagination of the public and, therefore, the sponsors.

Before examining the reasons for the modern upsurge in women's golf it is also worth looking at the way fashions in dress have changed, for these have had a great bearing on the pattern of growth. Victorian dress was inhibiting for lady golfers, but after World War I skirts became shorter and throughout the 1920s and 1930s were worn at around mid-calf height. Golfers wore thick woollen socks and sweaters and cardigans were also acceptable.

The first attack on this traditional garb occurred at the English Ladies' Championship of 1933 and was made in a quite, at that time, staggering fashion. The name of Gloria Minoprio does not feature in any roll of champions but her appearance on the first day of that event at Westward Ho! placed her name firmly in the headlines. She appeared on the 1st tee dressed in dark blue trousers with a matching blue jacket topped off by a blue turban. The trousers were exquisitely tailored and close-fitting and caused consternation in the ranks of the Ladies' Golf Union which issued a proclamation deploring any departure from the traditional costume of the game. In addition to her audacious dress, Miss Minoprio carried just one single club, a straight-faced cleek which she used on every shot, even putts. She was clearly an eccentric and after her inevitable first-round defeat she disappeared until the following year when she turned up again at the Championship in the same style of dress.

Miss Minoprio's breakthrough made slacks an acceptable form of dress for women on the course, and in America the women went a stage further. For the final of the 1947 British Women's Championship, Babe Zaharias had to be restrained from appearing in a pair of red and white checked shorts.

By 1970 prize-money on the LPGA Tour amounted to $750,000 for 21 events, but the Tour faced a financial crisis. It was rescued by the appearance of the giant Colgate corporation which saw the potential of the women's game and in 1972 started the first $100,000 tournament, the Colgate–Dinah Shore Winner's Circle. This marked the turning point in the fortunes of the LPGA; other sponsors followed with increased prize-money and this in turn attracted a phalanx

Above Laura Baugh, one of the early glamour girls on the LPGA Tour.

Right Jan Stephenson, cover girl and a leading money-winner on the LPGA Tour.

of young players who not only played the game well but looked good on the course. In 1975 the LPGA hired a marketing man, Ray Volpe, to act as the Commissioner for the Tour and within three years prize-money had risen to over $6 million.

Volpe sold the Tour on the glamour and sex-appeal of the younger players and the strategy worked. The Tour's first glamour-girl was Laura Baugh who in 1971, at the age of 16, had become the youngest winner of the US Amateur title and who turned professional in 1973. Laura Baugh was marketed like no other lady golfer had been before. Her obvious physical attractions adorned posters and calendars and she is said to have made over $1 million from endorsements even though she has yet to win a LPGA tournament. Laura Baugh was followed by Jan Stephenson, an Australian who also joined the Tour in 1973, and she too was promoted as a pin-up, sometimes in provocative poses which brought cries of

protest from the feminist movement.

Nonetheless, the formula worked. The corporate budgets were controlled by men and the money poured in. What the LPGA Tour needed now was a player who was not only attractive but could stamp her personality on the game through the excellence of her play. They found her in Nancy Lopez, a bubbly, dark-haired girl of Mexican extraction who had first caught the attention of the golfing public when she won the New Mexican Women's Amateur title at the age of 12. In 1977, at the age of 20, she turned professional and in her first full year on the Tour, 1978, rewrote the record books by winning eight times in America and also capturing the Colgate European event at Sunningdale. Her winnings for that year were $190,000 and the next year she won eight times and collected nearly $200,000.

Ten years after she turned professional Miss Lopez, now a mother of two children, captured her 35th LPGA

Nancy Lopez on her way into the record books during the 1978 season.

title at the beginning of 1987 and boosted her career winnings to nearly $2 million. She is not the leading career money-winner on the Tour, however. That honour goes to Pat Bradley who in 1986 won nearly $500,000 on the Tour and became the first player to win $2 million; she was joined on that mark by JoAnne Carner who, as JoAnne Gunderson, won the US Amateur five times. At the end of the 1986 season there were no less than 14 golfing dollar millionairesses, and with $11 million at stake annually there are likely to be a few more.

Obviously the climate in America made it easier for the players to appear in short skirts, or even short shorts, and the freer attitude to women golfers in that country also helped. Britain was much slower to accept that women could play the game well, and meanwhile anybody would find it difficult to look stunning clad in four sweaters and waterproof trousers. From its beginnings, golf in Britain was very much a masculine pastime. Clubhouses were built on austere lines with solid club furniture inside. Rooms were set aside for strictly male activities such as cards or snooker and women were not exactly made welcome. Very few clubhouses even had women's lavatories. Women golfers were tolerated but were regarded in much the same light as women drivers; indeed, in some quarters this attitude still prevails.

However, the rising standards of the game in the United States and the presence of American players at Sunningdale for the Colgate event brought about the creation of the Women's Professional Golfers' Association which was founded in 1979. Prize-money was small but at least a start had been made. Various political wranglings nearly put paid to the WPGA in 1982 – 83 but the organization was restructured under the aegis of the PGA and with Michelle Walker, herself one of the outstanding British players in recent times, as its new Chairman it came back from the brink. Prize-money for 1987 reached £1 million for the first time and the WPGA now has its own star player, Laura Davies.

Miss Davies turned professional in 1985 and her impact has been considerable. She is without doubt the longest hitter the women's game has ever seen, capable of hitting the ball more than 300 yards. This ability, coupled with an improving short game, enabled her to top the money-list in her first year with £21,000 in prize-money. In 1986 she finished top again with a late run which saw her win the British Ladies' Open Championship, an event started in 1976, plus the last tournament of the year. This enabled her to overhaul Sweden's Liselotte Neumann by about £500 with prize-money of £37,500. Today competition on the WPGA Tour is fierce and standards are rising rapidly. It may be some time before the British are able to compete with the Americans in any kind of international match but there is no doubt that the time will eventually come.

Women's golf has advanced further in the past decade than it did in the previous century and many male golfers now realize that the best lady professionals can provide a much clearer insight into technique than the musclemen of the male professional game. Very few male golfers could emulate the impact position of Greg Norman, for example, without the possibility of doing themselves a lasting injury. The qualities of timing and rhythm, which are essential if a woman is to hit the ball effectively, can more easily be assimilated by a male golfer.

The tweeds-and-brogues image of women's golf is now well and truly buried. Although some chauvinistic bastions remain, the citadel has been well and truly stormed and the emancipation of women golfers is now a reality.

Right Michelle Walker, for many years the leading British player.

Far right Kathy Baker, winner of the US Women's Open in 1985.

Laura Davies on her way to victory in the British Ladies' Open at Birkdale in 1986.

THE SENIORS

Few games offer the player such an extended run as golf. At a time when many other sportsmen are 'hanging up their boots', golfers can continue to enjoy the challenge of their game for as long as they are physically able to swing a club. Indeed, it has been recorded that a certain Nathaniel Vickers, an American, was still playing well after his 100th birthday, while as recently as 1985 a Swiss golfer named Otto Bucher set a new world record when, at the age of 99, he became the oldest player to hole-in-one.

So far as professional golf is concerned, the fastest growth over the past seven years has occurred on the American Senior Tour. This Tour is administered by the main US Tour and its expansion has been quite phenomenal. The idea for such a Tour had its beginnings in an event which began in 1978 and was called The Legends of Golf: a four-ball better-ball tournament for players who were over 50. It was televised and the ratings were reasonable, but then in 1979 the event really caught the imagination when there was a sudden-death play-off which lasted six holes before Roberto de Vicenzo and Julius Boros eventually won. As these elder statesmen traded birdies on every hole, the idea grew that they could not only still play the game pretty effectively but they could also provide a fair degree of entertainment.

Other factors also played a part. Firstly, at the end of 1979 Arnold Palmer reached the age of 50. The man who had brought golf to the masses in the early 1960s was still one of the best-known names in sport and it was not beyond the realms of possibility that he could provide the same impetus to a Senior Tour. Initially, Palmer was not too enthusiastic about becoming the figurehead of the new Tour, feeling that his competitive days on the main Tour had not run their full course, but he did agree that he would play in whatever events were arranged. There was also a feeling that the days of the superstar on the main US Tour were numbered. Such was the competition that it appeared unlikely that any group of players would establish the supremacy

that Palmer, Gary Player and Jack Nicklaus had enjoyed over the previous twenty years. All the big names in the game, with the exception of Tom Watson, were over 40 and finding it increasingly hard to keep up with the young bloods.

Thus the Senior Tour was born on the premise that since the superstars had attracted so much attention when they were in their prime, they might well do the same in their later years. The new Tour made a quiet start with just two events in 1980, followed by five in 1981, 11 in 1982, 18 in 1983, 24 in 1984, and 31 in 1986.

In 1987 the Seniors played for $7.5 million, available in 37 tournaments, a staggering rise unmatched in any other area of the professional game. The key to the Tour's financial success lies in the two-day pro-am event linked to every tournament in which 200 amateurs pay up to $4,500 to partner their old heroes. Most of these amateurs are in the same age group as the Seniors, as are the chairmen of the corporations which sponsor the events.

The success of the Senior Tour has brought a new lease of golfing life to those players who still had the skills but, because of their advancing years, could not keep up with the youngsters on the main Tour. The most successful senior player is 58-year-old Don January, a lean and languid Texan who won 12 times on the main Tour, including the 1967 US PGA Championship, and collected over $1 million in 24 years. In just seven years on the Senior Tour, January has won 25 times and collected another $1 million in career earnings so far. Another double dollar millionaire is Miller Barber, a man with a loop in his swing that only a mother could love. Barber won 11 times in his 16-year career on the main Tour but has won 19 times on the Senior Tour and at the age of 56 is likely to win again.

One of the most remarkable stories of the Senior Tour concerns the achievements of Australia's Peter Thomson. In his prime, Thomson was the master tactician of links courses and achieved five Open Championship victories. He was a craftsman who

Two of the most successful players on the Senior Tour. **Above** Don January. **Above right** Miller Barber.

Peter Thomson, now enjoying high earnings from the Senior Tour, tackles the Open at St Andrews in 1984.

manoeuvred the ball round the rugged terrain of St Andrews, Hoylake or Lytham, always seeking the best spot for the drive to finish, the best side of the green to land the ball. Like a chess grand master, he plotted and planned his way round the course and he simply could not abide the dartboard golf of America with its watered fairways and greens. Thomson made few trips to America and won only one tournament, the 1956 Texas Open. In 1979 he turned 50 and had virtually given up tournament golf and was concentrating on a career in politics. Defeated in an election for a seat in the Australian Senate, he decided in 1982 to try his luck on the Senior Tour. What attracted him to it was the fact that the courses were not the 7,000 yard (6,400 m) monsters he so abhorred; instead, the courses on the Senior Tour were no more than 6,500 yards (5,944 m) long and were chosen for their subtlety of design and the premium they placed on skilled shot-making. Thomson began to feel at home in America and in 1984 he won twice and earned over $200,000 in prize-money. In 1985 he totally dominated the Tour, winning nine tournaments and topping the money list with close on $400,000. Having never come close to being a dollar millionaire, not that he particularly

wanted to, Thomson is now close to achieving that status.

At the end of the 1986 season Thomson's position at the head of the Seniors had been taken over by another Australian, Bruce Crampton. Crampton retired from professional golf in 1977 having won 15 times on the main Tour and earned over $1 million. He went into the oil business but when at the end of 1985 his 50th birthday coincided with the world slump in oil prices, he ventured back into his original profession. It was a wise decision as Crampton won seven times in 1986 and pocketed nearly half a million dollars in the process.

The same year also saw the arrival of Gary Player on the Senior scene. He had in fact entered one event at the end of 1985 and won it, and in 1986 he added three more victories to bring his world-wide career total of wins to over 130. In his best year on the main Tour, Player won $177,000; in 1986 he won nearly $300,000. This litany of ever-increasing bank balances should not, however, detract from the performances of some of the less well-known players. Names such as Dale Douglass, Charles Owens and Walter Zembriski would not be on anybody's list of all-time greats yet they too are enjoying that same twilight rejuvenation. Douglass did win three times on the main Tour and played for the United States in the 1969 Ryder Cup but it took him 22 years to amass $500,000 in career earnings. In his first year on the Senior Tour he won four tournaments and over $300,000.

The stories of Owens and Zembriski are perhaps the most extraordinary. Owens, a 57-year-old black man, spent 20 years of his professional life as a golfing gypsy, playing the odd main Tour event and picking up cheques in regional tournaments. He has one permanently locked leg, the legacy of a parachuting accident while he was in the Army, while the other knee is minus a cartilage. He has an eye condition which can cause temporary blindness, and if all these physical ailments were not enough, he plays golf using a reverse-handed grip and putts with a 50 inch (1.27 m) long putter that weighs 3 pounds (1.3 kg). This unlikely combination enabled Owens to win over $200,000 on the Senior Tour in 1986 and he did that while travelling with a new-born baby who was not his grandchild but his daughter.

Zembriski was a steel construction worker for 11 years and learnt the game on a public course. He tried his luck on the main Tour but won nothing and reverted to playing in regional events. He turned 50 in 1985 and has now won well over $200,000.

Players such as Chi Chi Rodriguez, Billy Casper, Doug Sanders, Gene Littler, and overseas stars Harold Henning and Bob Charles are all clamouring for their share of the riches. At the end of 1986, Charles captured a cheque for $250,000 as his share of a victory in a mixed tournament in which the Seniors partnered lady professionals from the LPGA Tour. This win was more than Charles collected in his entire career on the European circuit.

The Senior Tour has now grown to such an extent that a qualifying school has had to be introduced for those players who cannot qualify on their past records, and it is likely that, as fields get larger, a half-way cut will take place. With the exception of Sir Stanley Matthews, who

was still nipping down the wing for Stoke City at the age of 48, there are no other comparable professional sportsmen still competing in their later years. While a mobile medical centre is on hand at each Senior Tour event, the chief agonies the players suffer are the same as they always were – errant drives and missed putts.

It is inevitable that a similar Tour will be created in Britain. The first move in this direction has already been made with the staging of the first British

Seniors Open at Turnberry in 1987, and a world senior circuit is a distinct possibility. However, before every professional in his late 40s starts honing his game for a début with the Seniors, a word of warning. On 21 January, 1990 a significant birthday will take place when a certain Jack William Nicklaus will reach the age of 50. That event will be preceded by Lee Trevino's 50th birthday in December 1989. Then life on the Senior Tour may just begin to get a little tougher.

Three colourful
characters from the
Senior Tour.
Left Chi Chi Rodriguez.
Above Doug Sanders.
Right Billy Casper.

GOLFING CELEBRITIES

The connection between golf and the world of entertainment goes back to the days of music-hall and variety. Copies of *Golf Illustrated* prior to World War I often depicted music-hall stars such as Dan Leno in action on the links and the Stage Golfing Society had a thriving membership. The nature of show business, whereby the entertaining was done at night, meant that there were long periods of day-time inactivity and golf provided an excellent alternative to the temptations of gambling on horses, drinking, or assignations with members of the opposite sex. Since professional golfers were also providing entertainment through their skills it was natural that there should be an affinity between the two professions, and show-business golfers are no different from other golfers in wanting to improve under the watchful eye of an acknowledged master.

It was in America, however, that the concept of linking a show-business name with a professional tournament first emerged when the Bing Crosby National Pro-Am was launched in 1937. Crosby was himself a scratch golfer, good enough to have played in the Amateur Championships of both Britain and America, and the idea of partnering the best professionals with famous show-business names gave the event immediate appeal. It was played over the three courses on the Monterey Peninsula, originally Pebble Beach and Cypress Point with Spyglass Hill being added later, and the crowds flocked to see their favourites from stage and screen in action. Crosby's old sparring partner, Bob Hope, also a single-figure handicap player, was a regular competitor and he too eventually lent his name to another US Tour event, the Bob Hope Desert Classic which began in 1960 in Palm Springs. The Crosby was staged over three courses so the Hope tournament went to four, the Crosby being played over 72 holes, the Hope over 90 holes. The main beneficiaries of these tournaments have been various charities and, in the case of the Hope, over $10 million has been raised in its history, most of which has gone to the Eisenhower Medical Centre in Palm Springs. The

Bing Crosby in company with Gary Player and Bruce Forsyth.

former President used to play in the event and his appearances helped to boost the crowds.

The money is raised in various forms but primarily from the amateur contestants who pay up to $10,000 to play; as there are over 400 of them, it all adds up to a great deal of money. Then there is the pre-tournament dinner where guests can share caviar with the stars, and the tournament programme in which various companies advertise and individuals pay to have their name in print as supporters of the tournament. All this is quite apart from the 50,000-odd spectators who pay to come and watch.

The result is the ultimate in golf razzle-dazzle, but in spite of all the fanfares and the fact that they are partnered by three amateurs, the professionals turn in some quite remarkable scores. The first winner of the Crosby was Sam Snead, while the Hope's inaugural winner was Arnold Palmer who won with a score which averaged a little over 67 for the five rounds. Palmer actually won the Hope five times but never won the Crosby.

Sometimes the publicity engendered by these tournaments was more a product of the celebrities' bad golf rather than the excellence of the professionals. Nothing hit the headlines quite like Spiro Agnew in the 1970 Hope Classic. The then Vice-President stepped onto the first tee in partnership with Doug Sanders and with his opening stroke hit the ball right in the middle of the club. Unfortunately, his sense of direction was somewhat awry and the ball caught Sanders on the side of the head while he was standing a few yards away. Down went Sanders with a deep gash on his head. But Agnew wasn't finished. He then started bombarding the crowd. One shot sent the gallery scattering on the left while the next removed several spectators on the right. The following year, the gallery was ready for him. Spectators arrived carrying placards which read 'Hit me first, Spiro' and 'Don't hit me Spiro, I voted for you'. He didn't disappoint them, sending one woman to hospital and making the rest of the gallery feel they

Bob Hope enjoying his golf in 1947.

Right Glen Campbell, another celebrity supporting his own event.

Two early British golfing celebrities.
Above right Douglas Bader, World War II hero and a very effective golfer on two tin legs, and (right) Sean Connery, an enthusiastic golfer in his own right and also winner as James Bond over Goldfinger in their memorable film encounter.

were taking part in some golfing form of Russian Roulette.

In the wake of the Crosby and Hope spectaculars, other stars began lending their names to US Tour events so that titles like the Dean Martin Tucson Open, the Sammy Davis Greater Hartford Open and the Andy Williams San Diego Open became familiar staging posts for the touring professionals.

In Britain, the show-business link with professional tournaments took much longer to become established, chiefly because televised golf was still in its infancy. The potential was there, however, as was demonstrated by a match held in the mid-1950s at Temple Golf Club, near Maidenhead, when Hope and Crosby teamed up against comedian Ted Ray and singer Donald Peers. So great were the crowds that the match had to be abandoned; the majority of the spectators knew very little about the game and were sitting on the greens tucking into picnic lunches. Temple, incidentally, was once the home club of Henry Cotton who held the distinction of being probably the only golf professional to top the bill in a variety show when he appeared at the London Coliseum in 1938 with a demonstration of his golfing skills.

Assisted by the boost Tony Jacklin had given to British golf with his wins in the Open and US Open, the televising of tournaments began its ascent and in 1974 it was decided that the coverage should be expanded. This decision saw the birth of the BBC Pro-Celebrity golf series which began in 1974 and, hosted by Peter Alliss, has been going strong ever since. Stars such as Sean Connery, Jimmy Tarbuck, Sir Harry Secombe and Bruce Forsyth had already proclaimed their love of the game, and it was felt that putting them on the course with well-known professionals might just provide a viable TV programme.

The series began at Turnberry with Peter Oosterhuis and Johnny Miller as the professionals and the stars came from both Britain and America. Purists winced at some of the swings displayed by the celebrities but there was no denying the programme's success as the ratings

soared to around 4 million viewers, an unheard-of number for a golf programme. It appeared that the programme appealed not so much to the dyed-in-the-wool golfer but to millions of non-golfers who liked to see their favourites performing at something for which they were not famous, and the scenic qualities of the game also had great appeal.

Stars such as Telly Savalas, Johnny Mathis, Bobby Charlton, Henry Cooper, Ronnie Corbett, Burt Lancaster, Jackie Stewart, James Hunt, Jack Lemmon, Val Doonican, Richie Benaud, Lew Hoad, Ted Dexter, Adam Faith, Terry Wogan, Jimmy Tarbuck, Bruce Forsyth and many others have appeared on the

show. The professionals have included Tony Jacklin, Peter Oosterhuis, Johnny Miller, Tom Weiskopf, Arnold Palmer, Gary Player, Lee Trevino, Severiano Ballesteros, Ben Crenshaw and Fuzzy Zoeller.

Some of the celebrities have played well, others not so well. Sean Connery is fiercely competitive but his swing is a little wooden, as is that of the left-handed Henry Cooper, but this is often so with people who take up the game later in life. Ted Dexter is a very fine golfer, good enough to win the President's Putter, while Jimmy Tarbuck, a member at both Coombe Hill and Wentworth, plays comfortably to a single-figure

Golfing celebrities on both sides of the Atlantic. **Far left** Telly Savalas. **Below left** Jimmy Tarbuck. **Below** Gerald Ford.

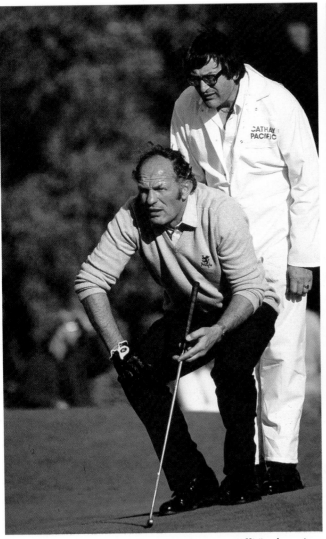

Henry Cooper.

Leading lady of British celebrity golf, Suzanne Danielle.

handicap. Snooker star Cliff Thorburn is another good player and Bobby Charlton has shown that the attributes of balance and poise that made him a legend for England and Manchester United are equally important in the golf swing.

The appearance of James Hunt, clad in a T-shirt, jeans and plimsolls, sparked a riot of angry letters about his appearance and also the presence of his large Alsatian, Oscar, who accompanied him during the match. His competitive instincts served him well, however, and even though he drove with an iron, he scored pretty effectively.

Of the others, Val Doonican plays to single figures at Beaconsfield and

Richie Benaud, not surprisingly, has a good eye for a ball. Telly Savalas has rather an ungainly swing and Eric Sykes is not too graceful, but every celebrity appeared as a budding Nicklaus when compared with the efforts of the unfortunate Peter Cook. One of the original stars of *Beyond the Fringe*, Cook was beyond redemption on the golf course and was hardly seen during the show as the camera lingered on clumps of gorse and bracken while the commentary informed the viewers that Cook was in there somewhere.

The main point about this series, though, is that it shows that the various celebrities are only human after all. While on stage they may be able to hold an

Johnny Mathis.

Terry Wogan.

audience of thousands in the palm of their hands, when it comes to holding a golf club they are just the same as everyone else. They too can slice, hook, fluff and three-putt and then suddenly produce the shot of a lifetime. It takes a good deal of nerve to set yourself up as a possible figure of ridicule in front of millions but this is what the celebrities do and the public admire them all the more for it.

Now the pro-celebrity scene is well-established in Britain with pro-ams being staged almost weekly. There is also a major PGA European Tour event, the Four Stars National Pro-Celebrity Tournament, which is supported by Terry Wogan, Jimmy Tarbuck, Henry Cooper and

Ronnie Corbett and is a 72-hole stroke-play tournament involving the leading Tour professionals in partnership with amateurs. This event and the celebrity pro-ams are aimed at raising money for various worthy causes such as Sunshine Coaches for handicapped children or the Stars Organization for Spastics. The combination of golf and show business has been very much a benevolent success story.

Novel transport for Victor Mature at the Four Stars Tournament, Moor Park, 1986.

FAMOUS CAREERS

ALLISS, PETER (b 1931)

Born in Berlin during his father Percy's spell as club professional at the fashionable Wannsee Club, he inherited his father's talent and during his career was considered to be one of the finest players Great Britain has ever produced.

He joined the professional ranks in 1946 after gaining international honours as an amateur. National Service in the RAF put a temporary brake on his progress and it was 1951 before he returned to golf. He was soon back in the limelight with a victory in the 1952 British Assistants' Championship and claimed his first title two years later by winning the Daks tournament. This was to be the first of over twenty professional tournament wins.

He was a fine long-iron player

who had superb poise and balance, combined with natural flair and power. A prolific winner, he captured five national titles and during one inspired spell was the holder of the Italian, Spanish and Portuguese championships at the same time. He also won the Vardon Trophy on two occasions, in 1964 and 1966.

His outstanding play during this era earned him Ryder Cup honours and he had a fine record, collecting several famous American scalps among them that of Arnold Palmer when the great man was at the very height of his powers.

After the 1969 Ryder Cup he

decided to retire from the professional game, and today his fine knowledge of the game coupled with a wry sense of humour have made him much in demand as a TV commentator both at home and abroad.

CAREER HIGHLIGHTS*

1956	Spanish Open
1958	Spanish Open
	Italian Open
	Portuguese Open
1961	Brazilian Open

ANDERSON, WILLIE (1878-1910)

As a teenager he emigrated from North Berwick just before the turn of the century and established a US Open record that has never been bettered, winning four times in 1901, 1903, 1904 and 1905. His feat was later equalled by Bobby Jones, Ben Hogan and Jack Nicklaus. He also came

second once, third once, fourth twice and fifth three times.

He established several scoring records during his career: 288 for a standard golf course in winning the Western Open in 1908 (one of his four victories in the event), and in the US Open he set a one-round record of 73 in 1904, lowering it to 72 the following year. Considering the courses and the

equipment of those days, these were great achievements.

CAREER HIGHLIGHTS

1901	US Open
1903	US Open
1904	US Open
1905	US Open

AOKI, ISAO (b 1942)

Renowned for his highly individual putting style, he has been one of the leading Japanese golfers for many years. His toe-up, heel-down putting action, coupled with a superb short game, helped him to become the joint record-holder for the lowest single-round score in the British Open with a 63 at Muirfield in 1980.

He has not confined his low-scoring feats to Britain and his homeland, where he has won over 40 tournaments. He is also a regular competitor on the US Tour where he has won once (the 1983 Hawaiian Open), and in the 1980 US Open he came within two shots of pipping Jack Nicklaus for the title.

His most notable achievements in Britain have been his victories in the 1978 World Match-Play Championship and the 1983 European Open.

CAREER HIGHLIGHTS

1978	World Match-Play
1983	European Open

*Career highlights include the 'Majors', national championships and the British PGA Match-Play and World Match-Play championships.

ARMOUR, TOMMY (1895–1968)

The 'Silver Scot', as he was known, achieved his greatest successes after going to live in America in the early Twenties. He also set a unique record of playing for both Britain and the US. He played for Britain in 1921 at Hoylake in the unofficial pre-Walker Cup match, then the following year played in the first official Walker Cup match, also for Britain. In 1926, as a professional, he then played for the USA at Wentworth in the last pre-Ryder Cup encounter.

He went on to win the US Open in 1927 and the US PGA in 1930, and returned to Carnoustie in 1931 to take the Open Championship. In later years he earned a glowing reputation in America as a teacher, although he was plagued with putting problems, inventing the term 'the

yips'. He was also the author of two highly successful instruction books.

CAREER HIGHLIGHTS

1927	US Open
1930	US PGA
1931	The Open

BALL, JOHN (1861–1940)

He was one of the game's finest early players and the only man other than Bobby Jones to win the British Amateur Championship and the British Open in the same year.

The British Amateur Championship did not begin until he was a well-established player, but when it did he quickly became a dominant figure in the event with wins in 1880, 1890 (his Open year), 1892, 1894, 1899, 1907, 1910 and 1912, giving a span of over two decades between his first and last victories. He continued to compete in the Amateur Championship until 1921, by which time he was 60 years old, but still he reached the sixth round.

Considered to be the equal in his day to Bobby Jones and Harry Vardon, he was a first-class shot-maker and a master craftsman with the whippy, hickory-shafted clubs of the day. One of his finest wins came in the 1912 Amateur when he found himself five down with only seven holes to play but he fought back and went on to win the Championship for the last time.

CAREER HIGHLIGHTS

1888	British Amateur
1890	British Amateur
	The Open
1892	British Amateur
1894	British Amateur
1899	British Amateur
1907	British Amateur
1909	PGA Match-Play
1910	British Amateur
1912	British Amateur

BALLESTEROS, SEVERIANO
(b 1957)

Unquestionably the finest natural talent to appear on the golf scene in the past 20 years, 'Seve' has already secured a place among the greats of the game. Born in a small fishing village in the north of Spain, he was the youngest of four brothers, all of them golfers. By the time he was eight years old, he had made his own golf club, using an old iron head and a stick, cut to length for the shaft. With this crude implement he was to develop the touch and skill that has become the hallmark of his game.

He first came to prominence during the 1976 British Open at Birkdale when his cavalier style of play produced some of the most exciting golf ever seen in the long history of the Championship. It took the 19-year-old Spaniard into a tie for second place with Jack Nicklaus, behind Johnny Miller. He continued to improve at a rapid pace with several top ten finishes in Tour events throughout Europe, and his first win came at Zandvoort in the 1976 Dutch Open, where he became the youngest player ever to win a European Tour event.

Over the next three seasons he began to dominate the game in Europe and in 1979 at Royal Lytham he realized one of the major goals of his career, capturing his first British Open title. He won again at St Andrews in 1984.

After his Lytham victory, he set his sights on America and in 1980 confirmed his status as an emerging superstar by winning the US Masters for the first time. He captured the Masters title again in 1983. He was, and still is, reluctant to commit himself to playing full-time on the US Tour, preferring to travel the world, competing in Japan, Australia, Europe and America.

He excels in both stroke-play and match-play formats, as his record in the World Match-Play Championship at Wentworth clearly shows with four victories since his first win in 1981. In the Ryder Cup he has been an inspiration to the European team and played a vital role in their historic win at The Belfry in 1985.

In 1986 he once again topped the European Order of Merit, thanks mainly to a devastating spell when he captured five consecutive tournaments and finished the season with over £200,000 in prize-money and a stroke average of 68.95.

CAREER HIGHLIGHTS

1976	Dutch Open
1977	French Open
	Swiss Open
	Japan Open
1978	Swiss Open
	Japan Open
	Scandinavian Open
	Kenya Open
	German Open
1979	The Open
1980	US Masters
	Dutch Open
1981	Australian PGA
	Spanish Open
	Scandinavian Open
	World Match-Play
1982	French Open
	World Match-Play
1983	US Masters
	Irish Open
1984	The Open
	World Match-Play
1985	Irish Open
	French Open
	Spanish Open
	World Match-Play
1986	Irish Open
	French Open
	Dutch Open

BARTON, PAM (1917–43)

One of Britain's most talented lady amateur golfers, she was sadly never to realize her talent fully. In World War II she was killed when the aeroplane in which she was flying crashed on take-off from RAF Manston.

A natural left-hander who was persuaded to play right-handed, she, along with Dorothy Campbell and Catherine Lacoste, had the rare distinction of holding both the British and American titles in the same year.

Her first major breakthrough came in 1934 when as a 17 year-old she won the French Championship. She finished runner-up in this event on three other occasions.

In 1934 and 1935 she reached the semi-final stages of the British Ladies' Amateur, and won the title the following year. This was her great year of triumph when she also won the US Ladies'. She won the British Ladies' again in 1939, then the war intervened causing her untimely death.

CAREER HIGHLIGHTS

1934	French Ladies' Amateur
1936	British Ladies' Amateur
	US Ladies' Amateur
1939	British Ladies' Amateur

BONALLACK, MICHAEL, OBE (b 1934)

Arguably the finest amateur golfer that Great Britain has produced in the modern era, he has won almost every honour the game has to offer. Throughout the Sixties and Seventies he was virtually unbeatable in Britain. Despite a rather ungainly swing, he won through thanks to a deadly short game and a superb putting touch.

Like Ted Dexter, another fine amateur golfer from the same generation, he had a flair for cricket. Unlike Dexter, who went on to captain England at the bat-and-ball game, he decided that golf was the game for him. His first major success came in 1952 when he won the Boys' Championship. Walker Cup

selection followed at the age of 22 and he was to become a regular member of the team over the next 20 years.

His record in the major British amateur championships in modern times is unsurpassed. Five British Amateur titles, three in succession from 1968 to 1970, five wins in the English Amateur and four English Stroke-Play titles bear witness to his golfing prowess.

The highlight of his distinguished career came in 1971 when he captained the Walker Cup team to a dramatic victory over the Americans at St Andrews. In the same year he was awarded the OBE for services to golf but increasing business commitments were beginning seriously to curtail his golfing activities. He then decided to concentrate his efforts on the

administration of the game, and this decision eventually brought him the coveted position he holds today as Secretary of the Royal and Ancient Golf Club at St Andrews.

CAREER HIGHLIGHTS

1961	British Amateur
1965	British Amateur
1968	British Amateur
1969	British Amatuer
1970	British Amateur

BOROS, JULIUS (b 1920)

He could be described as a late developer, but he lost no time once he got started. Of Hungarian extraction, he turned professional in 1950 at the age of 30 and joined the US Tour. He completed a magnificent hat-trick in 1952, winning the US Open, becoming Player of the Year and leading money-winner. He also won the Open title in 1963 when he was 43, the second oldest to take the crown. When the US PGA title came his way in 1968, it made him the oldest player to win a Major.

He was one of the most consistent players on the US Tour, passing $1 million in winnings in 1977. Strangely, he achieved this record with the minimum of practice, not wishing to subject himself to extra strain because of numerous ailments. He was four times a Ryder Cup player and won the US PGA Seniors in 1971.

CAREER HIGHLIGHTS

1952	US Open
1963	US Open
1968	US PGA

BRADSHAW, HARRY (b 1913)

He was one of a crop of fine Irish golfers who emerged in the early Forties. He is best remembered for his famous shot, played from a broken beer bottle, during the 1949 British Open at Royal St George's.

Golfing legend recalls that during the second round of the Championship he found that his ball had come to rest inside the remains of a broken beer bottle which had been left in the rough at the 5th hole. Although almost certain that he was entitled to a free drop, he decided to play the ball as it lay. The subsequent shot travelled only a few yards. Rounds of 68, 77, 68 and 70 left him in a tie for the title with Bobby Locke, but he was well beaten by the South African in the ensuing 36-hole play-off for the Championship.

Although he never came that close to winning the Open again, he was nevertheless a fine golfer who won the Irish Professional title on no less than 10 occasions. He also campaigned successfully on the mainland, winning the Dunlop Masters twice, in 1953 and 1955.

CAREER HIGHLIGHTS

1947   Irish Open
1949   Irish Open

BRAID, JAMES (1870-1950)

A member of golf's Great Triumvirate, along with J.H. Taylor and Harry Vardon, he was born in a small village on the shores of the Firth of Forth. His greatest achievements were in the British Open. He won the Championship five times and finished fifth or better on no fewer than 15 occasions.

As an amateur he worked as a clubmaker in London, then shot to fame in 1895 when he held the Open champion

of the day, J.H. Taylor, to a halved match. He turned professional and worked as club professional at Romford Golf Club in Essex. In 1904 he moved to Walton Heath, which he also helped to design, and he stayed at the beautiful Surrey course for the next forty years.

Winner of the inaugural PGA Match-Play Championship in 1903, Braid went on to win the event on three other occasions before 1907. He won the Championship again in 1911, and even in his late 50s was still a force to be reckoned with, reaching the final in 1927 when he lost to Archie Compston.

His first Open triumph came in 1901 after several near-misses. But once he had made the breakthrough he was to dominate the Championship to the same extent as his illustrious contemporaries, Taylor and Vardon.

A powerful swing and a calm temperament were his greatest assets. Regardless of the excitement around him, he always appeared outwardly calm and unperturbed.

CAREER HIGHLIGHTS

1901	The Open
1903	PGA Match-Play
1905	The Open
	PGA Match-Play
1906	The Open
1907	PGA Match-Play
1908	The Open
1910	The Open
	French Open
1911	PGA Match-Play

BROWN, ERIC (1925-86)

One of Britain's finest exponents of match-play golf, he relished the cut-and-thrust of man-to-man encounters and this was reflected in his distinguished Ryder Cup record, both as a player and as non-playing captain.

He had a fine amateur career which culminated in his winning the 1946 Scottish Amateur Championship, after which he turned professional.

His breakthrough in the paid ranks came in 1951 when he won the Swiss Open. He went on to collect four more international titles along with seven major tournament victories, including the 1957 Dunlop Masters. That year he enjoyed one of his finest Ryder Cup triumphs with an emphatic win over American tough-guy Tommy Bolt. His victory inspired the rest of the team and the result was a rare triumph for Great Britain and Ireland.

He captained the Ryder Cup team twice in a non-playing capacity: in 1959 at Royal Birkdale and in 1971 at St Louis, Missouri.

CAREER HIGHLIGHTS

1951	Swiss Open
1952	Italian Open
1953	Irish Open
	Portuguese Open
1960	PGA Match-Play
1962	PGA Match-Play

CARNER, JOANNE (b 1939)

She has proved to be one of the greats of women's golf with a brilliant career both as an amateur and a professional. She compiled one of the finest amateur records ever, capturing five US Amateur titles in 1957, 1960, 1962, 1966 and 1968, the US Girls' Junior in 1956 and she played in four Curtis Cup matches.

After turning pro in 1970 at the age of 30 she went from strength to strength, and to the end of the 1986 season had captured 42 tournament victories. She was twice winner of the US Open, in 1971 and 1976, which gave her the record of being the only woman to have won USGA Junior, US Amateur and US Women's Open titles. She has been the leading money-winner three times on the Tour, Player of the Year three times and five times winner of the Vare Trophy for the lowest scoring average.

She became the LPGA Tour's second player to top $2 million in winnings and was elected to the Hall of Fame in 1982 following her 35th win.

CAREER HIGHLIGHTS

1957	US Ladies' Amateur
1960	US Ladies' Amateur
1962	US Ladies' Amateur
1966	US Ladies' Amateur
1968	US Ladies' Amateur
1971	US Women's Open
1975	Australian Ladies' Open
1976	US Women's Open

CARR, JOE (b 1922)

In the era before Michael Bonallack he was the dominant figure in British amateur golf. His first victory came in 1941 in the East of Ireland Amateur Championship and thereafter he was never far from contention in almost every major amateur event over the next 30 years.

In his prime he had a typical Irish swing: full-blooded, free and seldom executed at less than full throttle. It was exciting to watch but it also took him to some of the more uncharted regions of the course. However, he was also blessed with excellent powers of recovery which often allowed him to turn what seemed like a certain bogey into a miraculous birdie.

He won more than 30 major amateur titles, including the British Amateur three times, in 1953, 1958 and 1960. He was a semi-finalist on three occasions and a beaten finalist in 1968 at the age of 46. All-conquering in his native Ireland, he was Irish Open champion four times in a ten-year period between 1946 and 1956. He was an automatic choice for the Walker Cup team between 1947 and 1965, and holds the record for the most number of appearances for a player from either country (10). In 1961 he reached the semi-final of the US Amateur Championship.

He often competed in professional events and produced several outstanding performances, the best being in 1960 at the Centenary Open at St Andrews when he finished eighth behind winner Kel Nagle of Australia. In Ireland, where he is treated as a living legend, he came close to winning the Dunlop Masters at Portmarnock in 1959; it took a blistering finish from Christy O'Connor to pip him for the title.

CAREER HIGHLIGHTS

1953	British Amateur
1958	British Amateur
1960	British Amateur

CASPER, BILLY (b 1931)

Consistency was perhaps the best club in his bag. He was never out of the top 60 on the US Tour from 1955 to 1976 and he became the second man after Arnold Palmer to top $1 million on the Tour. A somewhat uncolourful person, he was nevertheless one of the greatest putters ever, needing just 112 putts to win the 1959 US Open, one of his three major championship victories.

Given his financial success he might have been expected to win more Majors than he did. He was second three times in the US PGA while his highest finish in the Open Championship was fourth. The US Masters course at Augusta, with its fast undulating greens, did not really suit his game although he did win there in 1970 after a play-off with Gene Littler. However, his best win was in the 1966 US Open in San Francisco

against the formidable Palmer. With nine holes left he trailed by seven shots and was just looking for second spot. But Palmer shed strokes like confetti and they eventually tied. In the play-off Palmer led by four after nine only to fade again and let Casper in for his second title.

His total of 51 Tour victories

leaves him sixth behind Snead, Nicklaus, Hogan, Palmer and Nelson. He has also triumphed overseas, winning the Brazilian, Lancome, Italian and Mexican titles. He played in a record eight Ryder Cups from 1961 to 1975, and was US captain in 1979. He is now active on the US Seniors Tour.

CAREER HIGHLIGHTS

1958	Brazilian Open
1959	US Open
	Brazilian Open
1966	US Open
1967	Canadian Open
1970	US Masters
1975	Italian Open

CHARLES, BOB, OBE (b 1936)

The greatest left-hander the game has ever produced, he can also claim to be, like Billy Casper, one of golf's finest putters. Originally from New Zealand, his first

victory was in his native Open in 1954 which he won while still an amateur.

His first appearance in Britain was in 1961 and two years later he became the only 'lefty' to win the Open Championship. His victory at Royal Lytham came almost a year after he had left the European scene to concentrate on

playing in America, where he won five tournaments between 1963 and 1974.

The 1969 World Match-Play Championship was the stage for one of the most devastating demonstrations of his putting prowess. With only ten holes to play in the final against American Gene Littler, he was trailing. He then sank putts of 45, 25 and 50 feet to pull back to one down with one to play. At the 36th hole he struck again, this time holing from all of 25 feet to force a play-off which he won at the first extra hole.

His only other opportunity to win the British Open came earlier in 1969, again at Royal Lytham. However, on this occasion he had to be content with second place behind Tony Jacklin. Among his greatest successes in Europe were back-to-back victories in 1972 in the John Player Classic and the Dunlop Masters.

During the last few years he has competed successfully on the US Seniors

Tour and his sole 1986 victory, partnering US woman professional Amy Alcott, brought him a staggering $250,000 in prize money.

CAREER HIGHLIGHTS

1954	New Zealand Open
1962	Swiss Open
1963	The Open
1966	New Zealand Open
1968	Canadian Open
1969	World Match-Play
1970	New Zealand Open
1973	New Zealand Open
	South African Open
	Scandinavian Open
1974	Swiss Open

COLES, NEIL, MBE (b 1934)

If there is one swing in European professional golf which has stood the test of time, it is that of Neil Coles. His first victory as a professional came in 1955 and within six years he had established himself as a prominent money-winner on the European Tour, and over the next two decades was never out of the top twenty.

He was also the first man to take his career earnings through the £200,000 barrier. In the light of today's huge prize funds this may not seem a great

achievement but one has to remember that when he was in his prime the first prize was equivalent to 19th place in the present Tour. In all, he amassed some 27 major tournament wins and played in 40 Ryder Cup matches over 16 years, a remarkable record by any standards and one which the leading players of today will be hard pressed to surpass.

CAREER HIGHLIGHTS

1964	PGA Match-Play
1965	PGA Match-Play
1971	German Open
1973	Spanish Open
	PGA Match-Play

COTTON, HENRY, MBE (b 1907)

It is said that every tournament professional should pay a percentage of everything he earns to Henry Cotton, for he was the man who did more than any other to upgrade the status of the golf professional from that of lowly employee who was not permitted to enter the clubhouse, to the exalted status many of them enjoy today.

Educated at a public school in Dulwich, London, Henry Cotton broke the mould for professional golfers who previously came into the game either as former caddies or as the sons of existing professionals. He made his breakthrough in 1926 when he won the Kent Open for the first time. He quickly moved on to greater things and by 1929 had been selected for the Ryder Cup team. In 1930 he confirmed his position as one of Britain's leading professionals and the same year finished runner-up in the PGA Match-Play Championship. In 1931 he won the Dunlop Southport event, a victory he was to repeat the following year.

In 1934 at Sandwich he captured the first of his three Open titles. The foundations for this win were laid with two magnificent opening rounds of 67 and 65 (the latter giving the name to the famous Dunlop 65 golf ball); these gave Cotton a nine-stroke lead and although he faltered in the final round he recovered to win by five strokes.

At the Carnoustie Open in 1937

he faced the whole of the American Ryder Cup team who were in Britain for the Cup matches and despite foul weather during the final two rounds his straight hitting and fine long-iron play provided the platform for an outstanding victory. His final Open triumph, at Muirfield in 1948, heralded a gradual withdrawal from the major events and although he won the 1954 Penfold tournament at the age of 47, he had by then become an infrequent competitor on the circuit.

CAREER HIGHLIGHTS

1930	Belgian Open
1932	PGA Match-Play
1934	The Open
	Belgian Open
1936	Italian Open
1937	The Open
	German Open
	Czechoslovakian Open
1938	Belgian Open
	German Open
	Czechoslovakian Open
1939	German Open
1940	PGA Match-Play
1946	French Open
	PGA Match-Play
1947	French Open
1948	The Open

CRENSHAW, BEN (b 1952)

For someone who is judged to be one of the finest putters in professional golf, he should have a string of victories to his name. In fact the little Texan, once rated as a challenger to Jack Nicklaus's crown, has fallen short of what was expected of him after a glittering amateur career.

When he turned pro in 1973 he won his first event, the Texas Open, and by the end of nine events had amassed over $76,000 for 34th place on the Tour. Since then his winnings have topped $2 million but his victories total just 13. It was a similar story in major championships – until 1984 when he won the US Masters just as it seemed a big title would elude his grasp.

His record in the Open Championship has followed a similar pattern of near-misses. He is also an avid golf historian and collector of golf memorabilia.

CAREER HIGHLIGHTS

1976	Irish Open
1984	US Masters

DALY, FRED (b 1911)

His rise to fame was temporarily halted by World War II after winning the 1940 Irish Professional Championship. Some might have been bitter at losing those vital years but he promptly took up where he had left off, winning the Irish Professional championship again in 1946 and going on to take the Irish Open title in the same year. This double victory quickly established him on the British tournament scene and he further enhanced his reputation by finishing 8th in the 1946 Open.

His liking for the Open championship became even more apparent in 1947 when he took the title at Hoylake. The weather, unpredictable throughout the Championship, deteriorated just as Daly completed his final round and none of the others in contention were able to match his total of 293 which gave him victory by a single shot from Reg Horne and the American Frank Stranahan.

In 1948 he finished in second place behind Henry Cotton at Muirfield and at Troon in 1950 he retained his reputation as a gritty Open contender with a third-place finish behind South Africa's Bobby Locke.

He played in the Ryder Cup team on four occasions between 1947 and 1953 with a fair amount of success. A small man, he made up for any physical disadvantage by using a very heavy driver and developing a full, supple swing that produced long straight shots. His other great asset was a superb judgment of pace, something which always stood him in good stead on the big links greens of the Open Championship venues.

CAREER HIGHLIGHTS

1946	Irish Open
1947	The Open
	PGA Match-Play
1948	PGA Match-Play
1952	PGA Match-Play

DEMARET, JIMMY (1910-83)

Although he failed to win either the US Open or US PGA Championships, he stamped his mark on the US Masters, winning it three times. In 1940 he won by four shots, then a record, from Lloyd Mangrum and was first again in 1947 ahead of Byron Nelson and Frank Stranahan. When he won again in 1950 he became the first three-time winner.

His US Open record shows that he came close, being runner-up to Ben Hogan in 1948 then finishing one shot out of the 1957 play-off between Mayer and Middlecoff.

He joined the US Tour in 1938 after lifting the Texas PGA Championship five times consecutively from 1934. In his first year on the Tour he won the Los Angeles Open. In 1940 he won six events apart from the Masters and claimed another half-dozen in 1947 when he was leading money-winner and won the Vardon Trophy for the lowest stroke average.

He played in three Ryder Cups between 1947 and 1951, emerging with an unbeaten record, and he also represented the US in the 1961 World Cup. He had 44 tournament wins and was elected to the PGA Hall of Fame in 1960.

CAREER HIGHLIGHTS

1940	US Masters
1947	US Masters
1950	US Masters

FALDO, NICK (b 1957)

He is a natural athlete who, before he took up golf, was a keen cyclist and swimmer. He first became actively interested in golf while watching the Open Championship on TV and quickly developed a superb natural rhythm under the guidance of teaching professional Ian Connelly.

Following a distinguished amateur career in which he became the youngest winner of the English Amateur Championship at the age of 18 years and 8 days, he turned professional in 1976. The following year he won his first tournament, the Skol Lager individual and progressed rapidly to further victories, including three PGA Championship titles in 1978, 1980 and 1981.

In 1983 he won five times in Europe to top the money list and in 1984 broke through in America by winning the Heritage Classic. At this stage in his career he decided to make major changes to his swing under the tutelage of David Leadbetter, a Zimbabwe professional resident in Florida. It was an arduous process and he spent two years struggling with his game before any improvement emerged.

His determination was justified when he recorded his first victory for three years in the 1987 Spanish Open over the difficult Las Brisas course and then, at a wet and windy Muirfield for the 1987 Open Championship, the new swing stood up under extreme pressure as he completed his final round with 18 consecutive pars to take golf's most sought after title by one stroke.

CAREER HIGHLIGHTS

1983 French Open
 Swiss Open
1987 Spanish Open
 Open Championship

FAULKNER, MAX (b 1916)

One of the game's true eccentrics, his exceptional talent more than compensated for his outlandish clothes, the constant changes in the way he played and the different types of clubs he experimented with. At one time he claimed to have owned over 300 putters and used every one of them!

There was nothing strange about his Open Championship victory at Portrush in 1951 – except that he was signing autographs 'Max Faulkner, Open Champion' when there was still a round to play. However, his confidence was vindicated and he took the title two shots ahead of Antonio Cerda.

He was renowned for his straight driving and excellent long-iron play, and during his professional career he won eight major tournaments including three Spanish Open titles; at the age of 52 he won the Portuguese Open.

CAREER HIGHLIGHTS

1951	The Open
1952	Spanish Open
1953	Spanish Open
	PGA Match-Play
1957	Spanish Open
1968	Portuguese Open

FLOYD, RAY (b 1942)

Here is one man who can never be written off whenever a major championship comes around. Twice a winner of the US PGA, in 1969 and 1982, he won the US Masters once, in 1976, and collected his first US Open title in 1986; he now only needs an Open Championship to complete his set.

This sort of record contrasts with his playboy image during the early years of his pro career when a colourful night-life seemed more important than a good performance on the fairways. However, when he put his mind to golf he proved a fierce competitor who has only been out of the top sixty in the Tour money list three times since he joined in 1963. His career earnings are now approaching $3 million.

He shares with Jack Nicklaus the Masters low aggregate of 271, including 21 birdies and an eagle. He is a veteran of six Ryder Cup matches and a steady winner away from the US with victories in Brazil, Canada, Costa Rica, and South Africa where in 1982 he won the Sun City $1 million Challenge.

CAREER HIGHLIGHTS

1969	US PGA
1976	US Masters
1978	Brazilian Open
1982	US PGA
1986	US Open

GEIBERGER, AL (b 1937)

If he never hits another ball, he will be remembered as the first player to break 60 for a round in an official Tour event. It came on 10 June 1977 during the second round of the Memphis Classic at the Colonial Country Club, when he shot a 59 including 11 birdies and an eagle. *And* he had to sink an eight-foot birdie putt on the final hole to seal it.

But for that feat, Geiberger's only other real claim to fame was victory in the 1966 US PGA Championship, his only major win, but he has twice been second in the US Open, and has been five times in the top ten on the money list.

He played in the 1967 and 1975 Ryder Cups but ill-health has dogged him since the Seventies, requiring several operations. He now plays infrequently on the Tour.

CAREER HIGHLIGHTS

1966	US PGA

GRAHAM, DAVID (b 1946)

Although a native of Australia, he has played the majority of his golf in America. Among his many achievements since joining the US Tour is the unique distinction of being the only non-American to win both the American Open and PGA titles.

In the 1979 US PGA he won a dramatic play-off against Ben Crenshaw, holing two monster putts for halves on the first two extra holes and then making a birdie three at the next hole for victory. His final round of 67 in the 1981 US Open at Merion was considered by many to be one of the finest demonstrations of accuracy ever witnessed in a major championship. He had started the day three shots behind the leader George Burns, but his closing round swept him to a three-stroke victory. In 1976 he captured the World Match-Play title at Wentworth thanks to some remarkable putting that left American Hale Irwin dazed and defeated.

Sometimes described as rather a hard-nosed character, Graham has a machine-like swing that works very well for him. Since joining the US Tour in the early Seventies, he has won eight tournaments and finished in the top ten on numerous occasions. In recent years he has also become involved in designing golf clubs for a leading American manufacturer.

CAREER HIGHLIGHTS

1970	French Open
	Thailand Open
1976	World Match-Play
1977	Australian Open
1979	US PGA
1981	US Open

GREEN, HUBERT (b 1946)

He has one of the most unorthodox swings in golf but is a talented player and always one to be watched. He joined the US Tour in 1971 and usually wins one tournament each year. His best year so far was 1974 when he finished third on the money list after four wins, then in 1976 he joined the élite by winning three events in a row, the Doral Eastern Open, Greater Jacksonville Open and the Sea Pines Heritage Classic.

The first of his two Majors came with the 1977 US Open at Southern Hills, then he took the US PGA at Cherry Hills in 1985. He looked set to take the 1978 US Masters when he went into the final round with a three-shot lead, but Gary Player shot 64 and Green missed a 30-inch putt on the final hole to tie and finished runner-up with Tom Watson and Rod Funseth. He has finished third and fourth in the Open Championship and has won in Ireland and Japan. He has played in three Ryder Cups, in 1977, 1979 and 1985.

CAREER HIGHLIGHTS

1977	US Open
	Irish Open
1985	US PGA

HAGEN, WALTER (1892-1969)

Flamboyant, brash, colourful – such adjectives are commonly used to describe this former caddie who was a golfing giant before World War I and during the Twenties. He was also a pioneer, lifting the game out of its dull jacket-and-breeches era into an age of colourful clothes and noisy showmanship. He also broke down the social barriers between the

pro and the amateur.

Altogether he won 11 major championships, a record exceeded only by Jack Nicklaus and Bobby Jones, and he was extremely popular with the crowds, always happy to chat to fans between shots. He began competitive golf in 1912 and two years later won his first US Open. He won it again in 1919 after a play-off, but his greatest achievements came in the US PGA when it was a match-play event. From 1921 to 1927 he won the Championship five times, four in a row from 1924, was runner-up once and did not enter on the other occasion.

He also had a glowing record in the British Open, winning in 1922 at Sandwich, in 1924 at Hoylake, in 1928 at Sandwich again, and in 1929 at Muirfield; in addition he was runner-up to Arthur Havers at Troon in 1923, and came third another year – all this from 10 entries.

He was opposed to the way golf professionals were treated in Britain, not being allowed to change or eat in the clubhouse. At the 1922 Open he countered this by hiring a limousine for eating in and changing his shoes, and parked it in front of the Royal St George's clubhouse. A year later, when finishing second to Havers, Hagen refused to attend the presentation in the Troon clubhouse, inviting the crowd for a drink at a local pub instead. Although he never won another major victory after 1929, he remained a threat for some while but was eclipsed by Bobby Jones who clinched his Grand Slam in 1930.

CAREER HIGHLIGHTS

1914	US Open
1919	US Open
1921	US PGA
1922	The Open
1924	The Open
	US PGA
1925	US PGA
1926	US PGA
1927	US PGA
1928	The Open
1929	The Open

HILTON, HAROLD (1869-1942)

With four British Amateur titles, two British Opens and one US Amateur Championship to his credit, he certainly deserves his place among the greats of the game. His career spanned almost twenty-five years and he was a consistent winner from the 1890s until World War I.

Short in stature, he was a ferocious hitter with an all-out attacking style which at times seemed almost to swing him off his feet, but for all that he was a remarkably accurate golfer, especially with his woods.

He is one of three amateurs, along with John Ball and Bobby Jones, to win the Open Championship. His victory in 1892 had a special significance since it was the first time the Championship had been played over four rounds. That was at Muirfield. His second title came five years later at Hoylake when he won by a single shot from James Braid.

In 1913 he won the British Amateur title for the fourth time, and then crossed the Atlantic and claimed the US Amateur Championship in the same year.

CAREER HIGHLIGHTS

1892	The Open
1897	The Open
1900	British Amateur
1901	British Amateur
1911	British Amateur
	US Amateur
1913	British Amateur

HOGAN, BEN (b 1912)

One of the greatest names in golf, he won the Masters, the US Open and the British Open in the same year, 1953, on his way to nine major championships. It is argued that he only failed to win the US PGA that year because he was unable to get back from Carnoustie in time.

Although he achieved so much on the course, it was his bravery off it that increased his appeal among golf fans everywhere. On a foggy morning in February 1949 his car collided head-on with a bus on a road in Texas and he was left for dead, his legs mangled in the wreckage. He was eventually taken to hospital and many doubted if he would ever walk again, let alone play golf. But he proved he was made of stern stuff. He not only recovered, he was back playing the following January and tied with Sam Snead in the Los Angeles Open, only to lose the play-off.

That year he won the US Open in five rounds after another tie, retained it in 1951 and triumphed again in 1953. Together with his first victory in 1948, that was his fourth Open success. He had won the US PGA twice before his accident, in 1946 and 1948, while the US Masters fell to him in 1951 and 1953. His

success in winning all four Majors is matched only by Gene Sarazen, Jack Nicklaus and Gary Player.

Oddly, he was a late developer. A professional from the age of 17, he trod a long, hard road to the top but by constant practice he acquired what many feel was the perfect swing. He did not win his first tournament until he was 25 and it was another eight years before he took his first Major. However, he won 62 tournaments on the US Tour, was a member of four Ryder Cup teams, twice as US captain, and was elected to the PGA Hall of Fame in 1953.

CAREER HIGHLIGHTS

1946	US PGA
1948	US Open
	US PGA
1950	US Open
1951	US Open
	US Masters
1953	The Open
	US Open
	US Masters

IRWIN, HALE (b 1945)

When it comes to consistency few players are better equipped. Solidly competitive, he has won over 20 tournaments since turning professional in 1968 and has

topped $2 million in earnings.

His first big success was the 1971 Heritage Classic and his second came in the same tournament two years later. In 1974 he sprang something of a surprise by winning his first Major, the US Open at Winged Foot, by two shots. His only other Major success came in the 1979 US Open at Inverness, despite a final round of 75. That year he also led the Open Championship going into the final round at Royal Lytham, but he fell away behind Seve Ballesteros.

His best Open Championship finish is joint second with Andy Bean behind Tom Watson in 1983 at Birkdale. His biggest success in Britain came in the World Match-Play at Wentworth. In 1974, the same year as his US Open success, he took the title and retained it a year later. He was deprived of a hat-trick when David Graham beat him at the 38th hole in 1976. He has also played in four Ryder Cup teams.

CAREER HIGHLIGHTS

1974	US Open
	World Match-Play
1975	World Match-Play
1979	US Open

JACKLIN, TONY, OBE (b 1944)

For twelve glorious months, beginning in July 1969, he performed at a level of golfing excellence seldom achieved by even the greatest players the game has known. His dramatic victory at Royal Lytham and St Annes in the Open Championship, when he became the first British golfer since Max Faulkner to win the title, heralded not only his emergence at a truly world-class player, it also signalled a revival of the belief that Britain could still produce players to challenge and beat the very best. In the same year he played a vital role in the Ryder Cup, earning a halved match against the mighty Jack Nicklaus.

In June 1970, at Hazeltine National course in Minnesota, he confirmed his status when he became only the second British golfer after Ted Ray in 1920 to capture the US Open title. Sadly, however, just as the British Open

THE CHALLENGE OF GOLF

provided the stage for his greatest achievement, it was also the setting for what many believe was the beginning of his fall from grace.

The year after his triumph at Royal Lytham he began the defence of his title on the Old Course at St Andrews in spectacular fashion, racing to the turn in an amazing 29 strokes. A birdie at the 10th provided the perfect start for his homeward run but then the heavens opened and play had to be abandoned for the day. The following morning his special touch had deserted him, and although he finished a very creditable fifth behind Jack Nicklaus, he must have felt that a golden opportunity had passed him by. Further misfortune befell him in 1972 at Muirfield; on this occasion he was the victim of cruel luck and an inspired Lee Trevino.

Although he went on to win many more tournaments including a dramatic play-off win over Bernhard Langer in the 1982 PGA Championship, his putting touch had begun to deteriorate along with his appetite for the tough grind of the professional circuit. He retired from the tournament scene in the mid-1980s but was soon back in the spotlight again, this time as non-playing captain of the victorious European Ryder Cup team which he inspired to an historic win at The Belfry in 1985.

CAREER HIGHLIGHTS

1969	The Open
1970	US Open
1973	Italian Open
1974	Scandinavian Open
1979	German Open
	Venezuelan Open

JONES, BOBBY (1902–71)

The greatest amateur of all time, he reached the climax of his comparatively short yet highly successful career in 1930 when he completed the Grand Slam. He won the British Open and Amateur titles, then returned to America for a ticker-tape reception before going on to win both the US Open and Amateur Championships. It is safe to say that this feat will not be repeated.

He was virtually invincible during the period 1923–30 when he won 13 major champsionships (this was before the Masters and US PGA replaced the amateur championships of Britain and America as Grand Slam events). He took the US Amateur five times in seven years from 1924 and the US Open in 1923, 1926, 1929 and 1930. In addition he

became a firm favourite in Britain where he won the Open three times, in 1926, 1927 and 1930.

His 1927 Open win and his British Amateur success both came at St Andrews where, on his first visit in 1921, he had torn up his card in frustration. When he returned there in 1958 as captain of the American team for the inaugural world amateur team championship, he was given the freedom of the Burgh.

Incredibly, after his 1930 Grand Slam success, he retired at the tender age of 28. He then wrote articles on golf and made instructional films, and helped to design the course at Augusta National for the US Masters tournament.

CAREER HIGHLIGHTS

1923	US Open
1924	US Amateur
1925	US Amateur
1926	The Open
	US Open
1927	The Open
	US Amateur
1928	US Amateur
1929	US Open
1930	The Open
	British Amateur
	US Open
	US Amateur

LANGER, BERNHARD (b 1957)

His greatest claim to fame could well be that he is one of the few professional golfers to have successfully overcome the dreaded putting 'yips'. He persevered, when lesser men might have given up, and his salvation came in the shape of an old 'Bull's Eye' putter which he found in the pro shop at Sunningdale in 1980.

A few weeks later he became the first German to win a European Tour event when he took the Dunlop Masters title with rounds of 70,65,67 and 68, leading from start to finish and averaging 27.5 putts per round! His putting yips now under control, if not fully cured, he went from strength to strength and soon established himself as a major force in European golf.

In 1981 he made a strong bid for his first major title, finishing second in the British Open to America's Bill Rogers at Royal St George's. A few weeks later, he won the Bob Hope Classic at Moor Park and by then was gaining recognition as a fine golfter. He confirmed his great potential in 1985 when he won the US Masters at Augusta.

Now a regular competitor on the US Tour, his precision play is ideally suited to the tight American courses. His first US Tour victory was in the Sea Pines Heritage Classic and he is a regular top ten finisher.

He made his Ryder Cup début at Walton Heath in 1981 and played in 1983 and in the great win at The Belfry in 1985. Born in Bavaria, one of his proudest moments came in 1981 when he won his native German Open, a victory he repeated in 1985 and 1986.

CAREER HIGHLIGHTS

1980	Colombian Open
1981	German Open
1982	German Open
1983	Italian Open
1984	French Open
	Dutch Open
	Irish Open
1985	US Masters
	German Open
	European Open
1986	German Open

LEMA, TONY (1934–66)

He had all the qualities to become one of golf's greatest players, but his tragic death in an air crash at the age of 32 has left only question-marks. At the time of his death he was one of the top four players in the world and only two years before he had landed his only major championship, the Open at St Andrews. It was his first golf in Europe and therefore the first time he had set eyes on the Old Course.

He earned the nickname 'Champagne Tony' after fulfilling a promise to buy champagne for the Press on winning a tournament in America, but his early years on the US Tour were far from vintage stuff. He turned pro in 1955 and although he won his first event two years later he did not hit the high spots until 1962. He won three events that year then finished fourth in the money list in 1963 including second place behind Jack Nicklaus in the Masters and equal fifth in the US Open. He had an impeccable Ryder Cup record. In two matches he scored 9 points out of 11. He also reached the semi-finals of the World Match-Play in 1965, losing to Gary Player at the 37th.

CAREER HIGHLIGHTS

1964	The Open

LITTLE, LAWSON (1910-68)

Little by name but big by reputation, he was the scourge of amateur golf between the wars. In 1933 he reached the semi-finals of the US Amateur and this earned him selection for the US Walker Cup team.

Paying scant regard to the reputations of Britain's top players, he and Johnny Goodman thrashed Britain's best, Wethered and Tolley, by 8 and 6 and then he slammed Tolley 7 and 5 in the singles.

He was equally ruthless a few days later when he reached the Amateur Championship final at Prestwick, beating J. Wallace 14 and 13. He shot 66 in the morning and had scored 82 for 23 holes when the match finished.

Back in America, he took the US Amateur by 8 and 7. In 1935 he was in the British Amateur final at Royal Lytham where Dr William Tweddell held him to a one-hole margin. He again took the US Amateur title that year and was sixth in the Masters. He turned pro in 1936,

winning soon after and scoring seven wins in all. Although he won the US Open in 1940, beating Sarazen in a play-off, he did not become quite the top pro many thought he would.

CAREER HIGHLIGHTS

1934	British Amateur
	US Amateur
1935	British Amateur
	US Amateur
1936	Canadian Open
1940	US Open

LITTLER, GENE (b 1930)

A fine player who has been content to make a good living off the US Tour while spending as much time as possible with his family and his collection of vintage cars.

He nonetheless managed to win 29 Tour events and to top $1½ million in winnings since turning pro in 1954. He made the switch after winning the 1953 US Amateur and the 1954 San Diego Open.

His only Major title came in the 1961 US Open, and he was second in 1954. He tied with Billy Casper for the 1970 US Masters but lost the play-off, and he should have won the 1977 US PGA but he allowed Lanny Wadkins to catch him and lost the play-off. He is now active on the US Seniors Tour.

CAREER HIGHLIGHTS

1953	US Amateur
1961	US Open
1965	Canadian Open

LOCKE, BOBBY (1917–87)

One of the true stars of the game, Arthur D'Arcy Locke, along with Australian Peter Thomson, dominated the golfing world during the post-war era. He won the British Open on four occasions between 1949 and 1957, and in a career which spanned some fifty years he won 38 professional and amateur events in his native South Africa, 18 tournaments in Great Britain, 15 in America and five others overseas.

Always immaculately dressed in plus-fours, white shirt, tie, white cap and matching shoes, he was as meticulous about his play as he was about his appearance, never allowing himself to be rushed into an error. He was a master of the draw, hitting every shot to the right and then curving the ball back onto the target with radar-like accuracy. This was a technique he adopted when he first came to Britain, finding it enabled him to hit the ball further without hitting it harder.

Perhaps his most famous Open win was at St Andrews in 1957 when the Championship was televised for the first time. On the final green Locke marked his ball to allow a fellow competitor to putt out. However, he inadvertently replaced his ball in the wrong spot and in front of the TV cameras and thousands of spectators crowded round the green, he putted out to win. It was not until later that his error was noticed on a news film, but it was decided that as he had gained no benefit from the situation his victory should stand.

He made his first appearance in America in 1947 when he finished 14th in the Masters. Shortly after this he won his first US tournament, the Houston Invitational, then went on to become a consistent winner there over the next three years.

CAREER HIGHLIGHTS

1935	South African Open
1937	South African Open
1938	South African Open
	New Zealand Open
	Irish Open
1939	South African Open
1940	South African Open
1946	South African Open
1947	Canadian Open
1949	The Open
1950	The Open
	South African Open
1951	South African Open
1952	The Open
	French Open
1953	French Open
1954	German Open
	Swiss Open
	Egyptian Open
1957	The Open

LOPEZ, NANCY (b 1957)

When she won the New Mexico Amateur at the age of 12 it was obvious that here was a champion in the making. From that small beginning she has become one of the greatest women players of recent times. A bubbling, extrovert personality, she has been the dominant figure on the US

LPGA Tour since her first season in 1978 when she won five tournaments in a row and nine in all.

She finished number one that year, repeated the feat in 1979 and 1985 and has only been out of the top ten in the two years when her daughters were born, in 1983 and 1986. She represented America in the Curtis Cup before turning professional in 1977, and in her first pro tournament she came second in the Colgate European Open at Sunningdale, which she returned to win in 1978 and 1979.

At the start of the 1987 season she recorded her 35th victory on the LPGA Tour and this earned her a place in the LPGA Hall of Fame. She is fourth on the all-time money list with $1¾ million.

CAREER HIGHLIGHTS

1978	Women's European Open
	US LPGA
1979	Women's European Open

LYLE, SANDY, MBE (b 1958)

With only nine holes left to play in the 1985 Open Championship at Royal St George's, he was battling to get on terms with the leaders. Then two birdies on the 14th and 15th swept him to the head of the field. A dropped shot at the final hole meant a nerve-racking wait to see if anyone could catch him, but when Bernhard Langer's birdie attempt slipped by the 72nd hole, Lyle became the first British winner of the Championship since Tony Jacklin in 1969.

He has the perfect pedigree for a professional golfer. The son of club professional, Alex Lyle, he was swinging a golf club around Hawkstone Park almost as soon as he could walk, and as he progressed through the amateur ranks it became apparent that he had the potential to go right to the top.

He began his professional career by winning the 1977 Tour Qualifying School and his first victory came the following year when he won the Nigerian Open. It was the forerunner of many victories and he soon began to dominate European golf, finishing top of the PGA European Tour money list in 1979, 1980

and 1985. He made the breakthrough in America when he won the 1986 Greater Greensboro Open and then in 1987 he took the US Tour's most important title when he captured the Tournament Players' Championship.

A Walker Cup player in his amateur days, he made his Ryder Cup début in 1979 and has been a regular in the European team ever since.

CAREER HIGHLIGHTS

1978	Nigerian Open
1979	European Open
	Scandinavian Open
1981	French Open
1984	Italian Open
1985	The Open

MANGRUM, LLOYD (1914–73)

For 46 years he held or shared the record for the lowest round in the US Masters, having set the mark at 64 in finishing runner-up to Jimmy Demaret in 1940. His record was equalled by several players and finally passed by South Africa's Nick Price who shot 63 in 1986.

Having been pipped for that 1940 Major, he had to wait until 1946 before taking his only US Open, winning after one of the few 36-hole play-offs in US Open history. After rejoining the US Tour in 1946 he was always in the top ten money winners for the next nine years. In 1950 he tied for the US Open but lost the play-off, and was in the top four on three other occasions.

He rarely played in the British Open but competed in the Ryder Cup from 1949 to 1953, losing just two of his eight matches, and was US captain on the latter occasion. All told, he won 46 tournaments including 34 Tour events.

CAREER HIGHLIGHTS

1946   US Open

MARSH, GRAHAM, MBE (b 1944)

Formerly a maths teacher, he was runner-up in the 1967 Australian Amateur Championship and winner of the West Australian title before he turned professional in 1968. Since then 'Swampy', as he is known to his fellow pros, has become one of the most successful international players in the game, winning tournaments in all the major golfing countries.

In the 1970s he preferred to concentrate on the lucrative Asian and Far East circuits where he was the top money winner in 1972 and 1973. He won his first Japanese tournament in 1972, the first of 21 victories he was to achieve there over the next 10 years.

Brother of Australian wicket-keeper Rodney Marsh, his only win in America was the 1977 Heritage Classic, and although he finished 22nd in the money list that year, he now rarely appears on the US Tour. He joined the European Tour in 1979 and his most important victories in Europe have been the 1977 World Match-Play title and the 1981 European Open.

CAREER HIGHLIGHTS

1970	Swiss Open
1971	Indian Open
1972	Swiss Open
	German Open
1973	Indian Open
	Thailand Open
1974	Malaysian Open
1975	Malaysian Open
1977	World Match-Play
1979	Dutch Open
1981	European Open
1982	Australian PGA

MASSY, ARNAUD (1877–1958)

Probably the finest golfer that France has ever produced, he became the first non-Briton to win the Open Championship when he held off the challenge of J.H. Taylor at Hoylake in 1907. He also had the distinction of being the only Continental golfer to win the Open until Seve Ballesteros won at Royal Lytham in 1979.

A consistent performer in the Open, he finished fifth in 1905 at St Andrews and sixth at Muirfield in 1906, and he made a strong challenge to capture the title for a second time at Sandwich in 1911 when he tied with Harry Vardon, but lost the subsequent 36-hole play-off.

Back on home ground he was an even more formidable opponent, winning the French Open three times and beating Ted Ray and Harry Vardon in the process. His successes in Europe were numerous and included the French closed title in 1925 and 1926, the Belgian Open in 1910 and the Spanish Open on three occasions: 1911, 1927 and 1928.

CAREER HIGHLIGHTS

1906	French Open
1907	The Open
	French Open
1910	Belgian Open
1911	French Open
	Spanish Open
1927	Spanish Open
1928	Spanish Open

MIDDLECOFF, CARY (b 1921)

A qualified dentist who travelled the US Tour under the nickname 'Doc', he also knew how to extract tournament victories. In a professional career lasting from 1947 to the 1960s he secured 37 Tour wins which leaves him in seventh place in the all-time list.

After turning pro, he won a tournament in his first season and did so every year until 1961. In 1949 he won the first of two US Opens, winning by one shot from Clayton Heafner and Sam Snead. He won again in 1956, also by one shot from Julius Boros and Ben Hogan. He was labelled a slow player but this did not stop him winning the 1955 Masters which he dominated, finishing seven shots ahead of Hogan, then a record margin. He was also runner-up in the 1948 Masters to Claude Harmon and in the 1955 US PGA to Doug Ford.

He took part in the longest play-off in US Tour history, completing 11 holes against Lloyd Mangrum in the 1949 Motor City Open before darkness enforced an agreed halt. He also played in the 1953, 1955 and 1959 Ryder Cups.

CAREER HIGHLIGHTS

1949	US Open
1955	US Masters
1956	US Open

MILLER, JOHNNY (b 1947)

There was a time in the mid-Seventies when he almost made the bogey obsolete. From the 1973 US Open at Oakmont, which he won with a final round of 63, to his triumph in the 1976 British Open at Royal Birkdale, he strode the world of professional golf like a colossus.

In 1974 he won the first three US tournaments on his way to eight victories that year and first place in the money list. At one stage he produced 23 rounds of par or better, and even though he took two months off he returned with a similar set of performances. Four more wins came in 1975 during which he scored two rounds of 61. At Birkdale in 1976 Miller trailed a young Seve Ballesteros going into the final round but shot 66 to win by six strokes.

Having scaled the peaks and earned a fortune, he fell from grace and curtailed the number of tournaments he played. In 1979 he won the Lancome in Paris but over the past six years victories have been few and far between. He has

won 23 US Tour victories since turning professional in 1969 and was twice a member of America's Ryder Cup team.

CAREER HIGHLIGHTS

1973   US Open
1976   The Open

MORRIS, TOM, JUNIOR
(1851–75)

Perhaps the finest natural talent the game of golf has ever produced, and despite a tragically short career, he set playing and scoring records that are remarkable even by today's standards. The son of Tom Morris Senior, he was a golfing prodigy who by the time he reached the age of 13 had already beaten many leading professionals in a local tournament. To prove this victory was no flash in the pan, he went on to win another tournament at Carnoustie after a play-off against Willie Park and Bob Anderson, two of the leading players of the day.

At the age of 17 he won his first British Open, taking the title at Prestwick in 1868. He won again the

following year when his father finished runner-up. In 1870 he took the title for the third time in a row and thus won the Championship Belt outright.

There was no Championship the following year but in 1872 when the familiar claret jug was introduced as the new Open trophy, his was the first name to be engraved on it. Declining health meant that his best finish over the next three years was a solitary second place, and when his wife died in childbirth in 1875 it was felt that he lost heart.

He began to suffer from bouts of depression and to drink heavily, all of which contributed to his premature death at the age of 24. Some say his death was the result of a lung complaint while others claim the cause was a broken heart. However, one fact remains undisputed: as a golfer, he stood head and shoulders above his contemporaries, and his like was not seen again until the arrival of the Great Triumvirate many years later.

CAREER HIGHLIGHTS

1868	The Open
1869	The Open
1870	The Open
1872	The Open

MORRIS, TOM, SENIOR
(1821–1908)

'Old Tom', as he came to be known after the arrival of 'Young Tommy', began his career as an apprentice golf ball maker, employed by Allan Robertson who was the premier manufacturer of the 'featherie' golf ball. Although he was 39 years of age before the first British Open Championship was played, Old Tom won the title four times, his final victory coming when he was 46. He played in every Open Championship between 1860 and 1869 and his final appearance was at the age of 75.

When he was 30 he left his native St Andrews after a dispute with Allan Robertson, because he preferred to play with the new gutta percha ball in preference to the featherie. He moved to Prestwick on the west coast of Scotland and it was there that he narrowly missed becoming the first ever winner of the Open Championship in 1860, finishing runner-up to Willie Park. He returned to St Andrews in 1864 to become the town's first golf professional and greenkeeper, a post he held for many years.

CAREER HIGHLIGHTS

1861	The Open
1862	The Open
1864	The Open
1867	The Open

NAGLE, KEL (b 1920)

Winner of the 1960 Centenary Open at St Andrews, he was 29 before he won his first important event, the 1949 Australian PGA, having turned professional three years earlier. At that stage in his career he was known as a long hitter but a poor putter, and he made little impact over the next few seasons. Gradually he improved his putting and became one of Australia's most consistent players, winning the New Zealand Open on seven occasions between 1957 and 1969.

He first came to Britain in the early 1950s and had little success, although he did achieve international acclaim partnering his fellow-countryman, Peter Thomson, to victory in the World Cup on two occasions, in 1954 and 1959.

His British Open victory, at the age of 40, was hard won with two world-class players, Arnold Palmer and Roberto de Vicenzo, hard on his heels throughout the final day. After that win he was never far from contention in the Championship, finishing fifth the following year and second at Troon in 1962 behind Arnold Palmer.

He won the Canadian Open in 1964 and tied with Gary Player in the 1965 US Open before losing the play-off. From being a man who did not like to travel too far from home, he became a fine international golfer with 10 wins in Europe between 1960 and 1971. In Australia he won a total of 21 events.

CAREER HIGHLIGHTS

1949	Australian PGA
1954	Australian PGA
1957	New Zealand Open
1958	Australian PGA
	New Zealand Open
1959	Australian Open
	Australian PGA
1960	The Open
1961	French Open
1962	New Zealand Open
1964	New Zealand Open
1965	Australian PGA
1967	New Zealand Open
1968	Australian PGA
	New Zealand Open
1969	New Zealand Open

NELSON, BYRON (b 1912)

A legendary figure, his name is spoken among golfers with awe and reverence in the same way as those of Nicklaus and Palmer. His fame stemmed from an astonishing record before and during the period of World War II. In 1944 he won 13 out of 23 tournaments and the following year he demolished all American records by winning 18 events including 11 in a row between 11 March and 4 August.

This record stands today. There are critics who are disparaging about it because many other top players were away on war service while Nelson, a haemophiliac, was exempted from military duties and so was able to play. Yet the fact remains that he scored 19 consecutive sub-70 rounds and had a stroke average for the season of 68.33.

He also won five major championships, beginning with the Masters, twice, in 1937 when he came

from four behind Ralph Guldahl to win by two shots, and in 1942 when he beat Ben Hogan in a play-off. His US Open win came in 1939 at Philadelphia after a three-way tie with Craig Wood and Densmore Shute. He and Wood tied with 68s as Shute was eliminated, then in a second 18-hole play-off he won by three after holing a full 1-iron for an eagle at the 4th. In the US PGA, he reached the final five times in seven years including three in succession from 1939. He beat Sam Snead in 1940 and Sam Byrd in 1945 but lost the other three.

He made only two British Open appearances, finishing fifth behind Henry Cotton in 1937 at Muirfield and playing in the 1955 event at St Andrews when Peter Thomson triumphed. That year he won the French Open at the age of 43. A former caddie, he has been an influential teacher and was the mentor of Tom Watson. He was also non-playing captain of the successful US Ryder Cup team at Birkdale in 1965.

CAREER HIGHLIGHTS

1937	US Masters
1939	US Open
1940	US PGA
1942	US Masters
1945	US PGA
	Canadian Open
1955	French Open

NICKLAUS, JACK (b 1940)

He is without doubt the greatest golfer of the modern game with 18 major championship victories – 20 if you include two US Amateur titles. He has won the Masters six times, the US PGA five times, the US Open four times and the British Open three times. It is a record unsurpassed, eclipsing such former greats as Ben Hogan, Walter Hagen, Bobby Jones and Sam Snead, and one which is unlikely to be equalled.

His amateur crowns came in 1959 and 1961, and he further underlined his potential in 1960 when finishing second to Arnold Palmer in the US Open. After turning pro in late 1961, it took him only a matter of months to win his first US Open, beating Palmer, then the great

American hero, in a play-off. Since then he has stamped his seal on the Majors to such an extent that he has completed the 'set' of four on three occasions. Only three other golfers – Hogan, Sarazen and Player – have completed 'sets', then only once each.

Up to the end of 1986, he had 71 US Tour victories to his credit, which is second only to Snead's 84, while his career earnings of almost $5 million are way out in front. Eight times he finished top of the money list and on only two occasions, in 1962 and 1979, has he failed to earn at least $100,000 in a year.

He has also been a prolific winner outside America with 18 titles including the World Match-Play in 1970 and six Australian Open titles. He played in six Ryder Cup matches and has twice been non-playing captain, in 1983 and 1987. Throughout his career he has acquired nicknames, beginning with 'Ohio Fats' when he was a raw, chunky youngster with a crew cut. Now he is affectionately

CAREER HIGHLIGHTS

1959	US Amateur
1961	US Amateur
1962	US Open
1963	US Masters
	US PGA
1964	Australian Open
1965	US Masters
1966	The Open
	US Masters
1967	US Open
	Australian Open
1970	The Open
	World Match-Play
1971	US PGA
	Australian Open
1972	US Open
	US Masters
1973	US PGA
1975	US Masters
	US PGA
	Australian Open
1976	Australian Open
1978	The Open
	Australian Open
1980	US Open
	US PGA
1986	US Masters

known as the 'Golden Bear'. He has trimmed his tournament appearances in recent years to concentrate on his businesses which include golf course construction in at least a dozen countries.

NORMAN, GREG (b 1955)

He did not become interested in playing golf until he was 17, preferring to caddy for his mother who was a keen player. However, once he was bitten by the golfing bug, he became a scratch player in just two years. He was a natural golfer and

success was to come quickly to the big blond Australian, now known throughout the golfing world as the 'Great White Shark'.

He turned professional in 1976 and after four events landed his first win, the West Lake Classic; after just six professional appearances he was chosen to represent Australia in the World Cup. In his first season in Europe, in 1977, he won the Martini tournament and finished 20th in the Order of Merit. Over the next few years he began to assert himself as a major

force not only in Europe but also the Far East and in his native Australia.

Along with Seve Ballesteros, he was the top attraction on the European Tour, and it was a logical move to test his mettle in America. With his big-hitting and positive style of play, he was an instant hit with the American golf fans and in 1983 he became a regular member of the US Tour, leading the money list in 1986.

Also in 1986 he played himself into a strong position in each of the Majors. He missed out at Augusta to Jack Nicklaus, led the US Open going into the final round, and had victory in the US PGA snatched from his grasp when Bob Tway holed out from a greenside bunker at the 72nd hole. He nevertheless captured his first Major that year when he won the British Open championship at Turnberry in convincing style. He also excels in match-play golf and has won the World Match-Play three times.

CAREER HIGHLIGHTS

1979	Hong Kong Open
1980	Australian Open
	Scandinavian Open
	French Open
	World Match-Play
1983	World Match-Play
1984	Canadian Open
	Australian PGA
1985	Australian Open
	Australian PGA
1986	The Open
	European Open
	World Match-Play

O'CONNOR, CHRISTY, SENIOR
(b 1924)

Known affectionately to every golfer in his native Ireland as simply 'Yer Man', he has resolutely withstood the test of time. While many of his contemporaries have long since given up competitive golf, he, like vintage wine, improves with age. He demonstrated this admirably in 1982 when, aged 57, he won the Seniors Championship for a record fifth time. Perhaps the secret of his staying power can be found in his swing; smooth and unhurried, with much of the power

provided by his strong hand action and superb timing.

He made his début in Great Britain in 1954 when he took Henry Cotton to the 23rd hole in the semi-final of the PGA Match-Play. Two years later he claimed the first of his numerous tournament victories when he won the Swallow Penfold. He was the first golfer to win a cheque for £1,000 in a British tournament, though his biggest pay-day by far was the then record £25,000 first prize in the 1970 John Player Classic at Hollinwell.

Although strongly tipped as a potential Open champion, he was never quite able to make the breakthrough, his best finish being in 1958 when he took third place at Royal Lytham. A Ryder Cup regular, he compiled an excellent record, playing in every match between 1955 and 1973. In all, he won 24 European events in his career before joining the Seniors Tour.

CAREER HIGHLIGHTS

1957	PGA Match-Play

OOSTERHUIS, PETER (b 1948)

After an outstanding amateur career which included successes in the Berkshire Trophy and the British Youths as well as selection for the Walker Cup team, he turned professional in 1968. Two years later he won his first pro event, the Young Professionals' Championship, and climbed to seventh place in the 1970 Order of Merit table.

He dominated the British golf scene in the early 1970s, leading the Merit Table and winning the Vardon Trophy for the lowest stroke average in four consecutive seasons. In 1972 he finished in the top ten on no less than 17 occasions in 19 tournaments.

After conquering Europe he set his sights on America and in 1973 came close to winning the US Masters at Augusta when he found himself leading the field by three shots going into the final round. Unfortunately, a closing 74 dropped him back into third place but nevertheless his overall performance persuaded him to compete regularly on the US Tour and in 1975 he left Britain to live and play in America. His one major victory since then was in the 1981 Canadian Open.

CAREER HIGHLIGHTS

1973	French Open
1974	French Open
	Italian Open
1981	Canadian Open

PALMER, ARNOLD (b 1929)

Jack Nicklaus may have won more titles but Arnold Palmer is the golfer who commands the most respect among the game's followers. He is generally credited with doing more than anyone to revive American interest in the British Open and setting it on the road to its present status.

His first Open appearance was in the centenary event at St Andrews in 1960, and he finished second behind Australia's Kel Nagle. He won the following year at Royal Birkdale and again in 1962 at Troon, a second and two firsts in three years. In all he has won seven Majors and one US Amateur, and but for

the arrival of Nicklaus in the early Sixties he would probably have won many more.

Ironically his only US Open success came in 1960 when he pipped Nicklaus, then an amateur, by one shot at Cherry Hills. This win followed weeks after his second Masters triumph and established him as a golfing great. At that time he drew vast crowds wherever he played and these became known as 'Arnie's Army'. However, even they could not inspire him to a US PGA victory, the only Major to elude his grasp, although he finished second three times. Today he still commands a vast following wherever he goes although he spends most of his playing days on the US Seniors Tour.

He was four times the leading money winner on the US Tour and was the first player, in 1968, to pass $1 million in career earnings. His 61 US victories leave him fourth on the all-time list while he also won 19 times overseas including two World Match-Play titles, one British PGA, one Australian Open and one Spanish Open. He was a member of six US Ryder Cup teams and non-playing captain in 1975. In 1974 he was elected to the World Golf Hall of Fame and in 1980 to the PGA Hall of Fame, a year after being awarded honorary membership of the R & A.

CAREER HIGHLIGHTS

1954	US Amateur
1955	Canadian Open
1958	US Masters
1960	US Open
	US Masters
1961	The Open
1962	The Open
	US Masters
1964	US Masters
	World Match-Play
1966	Australian Open
1967	World Match-Play
1975	Spanish Open

PATE, JERRY (b 1953)

For someone who enjoyed such a glowing amateur career and a magical start in the professional ranks, he could have expected to have amassed more tournament victories then eight on the US Tour plus one in Japan. But he has earned $1½ million and has done so despite a severe neck muscle injury and subsequent torn shoulder cartilage which required surgery and curtailed his play.

His brilliant amateur career included victory in the 1974 US Amateur Championship, equal first place in the individual in the World Amateur Team Championship and a Walker Cup place in 1975. His first year as a professional, 1976, was full of glittering prizes, none more so than the US Open at Atlanta where he beat Tom Weiskopf and Al Geiberger by two shots. He followed up

with the Canadian Open on his way to finishing 10th in the money list. He came to grief at Royal Birkdale in the British Open, however, slumping to an 87 in the third round.

Only once since 1976 has he come close to winning another Major, three-putting the final green in the US PGA at Oakmont in 1978 to tie with Tom Watson and John Mahaffey then losing the play-off. Between 1978 and 1982 he was never out of the top eleven in the money list, and at 27 he became the youngest player to reach $1 million in winnings. Since then he has struggled to recapture his earlier form.

CAREER HIGHLIGHTS

1974	US Amateur
1976	US Open
	Canadian Open
1980	Brazilian Open

PLAYER, GARY (b 1935)

Pound for pound, he is the finest golfer of the modern era. Standing only 5ft 7in (1.70m) tall and weighing 150 lb (68 kg), his greatest assets have been his excellent physical condition and sheer determination to succeed.

He first visited Britain in 1955 and was criticized by many of his fellow professionals for having a bad grip, a faulty stance and various other technical deficiencies. These criticisms served only to harden Player's resolve to succeed and he won his first title that same year, defeating fellow South African Harold Henning in the final of the Egyptian Match-Play Championship.

The first of his three Open wins came in 1959 at Muirfield when he stormed through the field with a final round of 68. He had already made his presence felt in America where he won the Kentucky Derby Open and he was well on his way to becoming the third member of the 'Big Three' along with Arnold Palmer and Jack Nicklaus. In 1961 he topped the US money list and won the US Masters in a dramatic struggle with Arnold Palmer. The following year he won his third major title, the US PGA, becoming the first overseas player to do so. In 1965 he joined an elite band of golfers, including Jack Nicklaus, Gene Sarazen and Ben Hogan, when he captured the US Open and went into the record books for winning all four of the game's major titles.

He kept up a hard globe-trotting schedule, jetting between the golfing capitals of the world without any noticeable effect on his health or form. His determination continued to serve him well, especially in match-play situations. Five times a winner of the World Match-Play Championship, his most famous victory was in 1965 against Tony Lema when he fought back from a seemingly hopeless position of seven down with only 17 holes to play.

His list of achievements compares favourably with anyone's. In the Majors he has won three British Opens, three US Masters, one US Open and two US PGA titles. Around the world he has

won more than 120 tournaments, and since joining the Seniors Tour he has added steadily to his haul.

CAREER HIGHLIGHTS

1956	South African Open
1957	Australian PGA
1958	Australian Open
1959	The Open
1960	South African Open
1961	US Masters
1962	US PGA
	Australian Open
1963	Australian Open
1965	US Open
	South African Open
	Australian Open
	World Match-Play
1966	South African Open
	World Match-Play
1967	South African Open
1968	The Open
	South African Open
	World Match-Play
1969	South African Open
	Australian Open
1970	Australian Open
1971	World Match-Play
1972	US PGA
	South African Open
	Brazilian Open
1973	World Match-Play
1974	The Open
	US Masters
	Australian Open
	Brazilian Open
1975	South African Open
1976	South African Open
1977	South African Open
1978	US Masters
1979	South African Open
1980	Chile Open
	Ivory Coast Open
1981	South African Open

RAY, TED (1877-1943)

With Harry Vardon and Tony Jacklin, he is one of only three British golfers to have won both the US and British Open Championships. A tall, powerfully built man, he hit the ball huge distances with a violent action that almost swung him off his feet, yet he never lost his grip on the pipe he kept firmly clenched between his teeth while playing.

He first came to prominence in 1903 in the final of the PGA Match-Play when he finished runner-up to James Braid, and by 1907 he was becoming a serious challenger for the Open title which he eventually won in 1912 after a series of high finishes over the previous six years. His US Open victory came in 1920 at the Inverness Club, Ohio. As the Championship neared its climax, it appeared that Harry Vardon was heading for a comfortable win but Ray finished strongly to snatch the title by a single shot from Vardon, Jack Burke, Leo Diegel and Jock Hutchison. His victory was the last by a Briton until Tony Jacklin won at Hazeltine in 1970.

CAREER HIGHLIGHTS

1912	The Open
1920	US Open

REES, DAI, CBE (1931-83)

Standing only 5ft 7in (1.70 m) tall, he was on the short side for a top-class golfer (Gary Player being the most notable exception), but whatever he may have lacked in inches, the little Welshman more than made up for in fighting qualities and skill. He had a full-flowing swing and throughout his career used a

double-handed or hammer grip, which was unique among the top professionals of his day. The 21 tournament wins he recorded in his career confirm his position among the great British players.

He first made his name in the PGA Match-Play Championship of 1936 when, after being five down with only 12 holes to play against Ernest Whitcombe, he fought back to win. In all he won four Match-Play titles, in 1936, 1938, 1949 and 1950, and reached the final on three other occasions, in 1953, 1967 and 1969.

Along with Abe Mitchell, he was probably the best British golfer not to win the Open Championship. On several occasions he seemed to have the title within his grasp, only to see his chance

slip away in the final round. He came closest to winning in 1954 at Birkdale, coming to the final hole requiring a par to tie. He hit a good approach shot which ran just through the green, but he failed to get down in two more shots and finished in second place behind Peter Thomson of Australia.

He was a Ryder Cup regular

throughout his career and he captained the team as a player in four matches between 1955 and 1961, and was also non-playing captain in 1967. Age proved no barrier to success, as he proved at the age of 60, tieing for second place in the 1973 Martini Tournament.

CAREER HIGHLIGHTS

1936	PGA Match-Play
1938	PGA Match-Play
1948	Irish Open
1949	PGA Match-Play
1950	PGA Match-Play
1954	Belgian Open
	Egyptian Open
1956	Swiss Open
1959	Swiss Open
1963	Swiss Open

ROBERTSON, ALLAN (1815-58)

It is difficult to assess his talents as a player for he never had the opportunity to compete in the Open Championship which was first played in 1860, two years after his death. However, the records which are available show that he was undoubtedly the outstanding player of his

time. It has even been suggested that the Open was instigated after his death to find the best golfer; while he was alive there had been no doubt about who was number one.

There was great rivalry between him and Tom Morris Senior, both on and off the course. Morris, who was an apprentice 'featherie' maker working for Robertson, left to manufacture the new gutta percha ball in competition with his former employer – something which Robertson saw as a threat to his livelihood.

Before their disagreement the two men often partnered each other in matches against other top names of the day. Robertson was the first man to break 80 around the famous Old Course at St Andrews and when he eventually conceded that gutta percha golf balls had come to stay, he was among the first to investigate the difference they would make to the game, including the need for iron clubs to play approach shots to the greens.

SARAZEN, GENE (b 1902)

A dapper little man in plus-fours, he was born Eugene Saraceni but changed his name because he felt it sounded as if he should be playing a violin. His golfing career spanned half a century, from Vardon to Nicklaus, but despite all his success it was one shot that put him on the map with British golf fans.

In 1973 he accepted an invitation, as a former champion, to play in the Open at Troon. He was then aged 71 and the Championship marked the 50th anniversary of his first appearance in the Open at the same venue when, as the latest star of the American scene, he failed to qualify. This time, playing with two other ex-champions, Fred Daly and Max Faulkner, he holed his tee shot at the Postage Stamp 8th and the TV cameras were there to record it.

A natural golfer, he won the first of his two US Open titles in 1922 at the age of 20 and a couple of months later added the US PGA title. He retained this the following year, inflicting on Walter Hagen his only defeat in five successive

finals. A barren spell followed but in 1932 he returned to Britain to win the Open Championship on the only occasion it has been held at Prince's, Sandwich. He also won the US Open that year, then in 1933 he triumphed in the US PGA for the third time.

His only Masters crown came in 1935: sinking an albatross two at the long 15th, he was able to catch Craig Wood and then won the play-off. This victory also made him the first man to complete a 'set' of Major titles. He played in six successive Ryder Cups from 1927, losing only once in the singles, then met with further success in the Seniors competitions. He is also generally credited with inventing the sand wedge.

CAREER HIGHLIGHTS

1922	US Open
	US PGA
1923	US PGA
1932	The Open
	US Open
1933	US PGA
1935	US Masters
1936	Australian Open

SMITH, HORTON (1908-63)

In the winter of 1928–29 he burst on the US tournament scene. He won eight of the nine events, a record which earned him a place in Walter Hagen's American Ryder Cup team. Although he won his singles it was not enough to prevent Britain winning 7–5. However, he maintained an unbeaten record through two more Ryder Cups, in 1933 and 1935, and was chosen again in 1939 and 1941 only for World War II to prevent either match being played.

After his dramatic arrival he was a regular winner over the following ten years and is remembered as being the first winner of the US Masters in 1934. In 1936 he won again, making up seven shots on Harry Cooper to win by one. He was third in the 1930 US Open behind Bobby Jones and Macdonald Smith, joint third the same year in the Open Championship at Hoylake and third again in the 1940 US Open, one shot outside the Sarazen-Little play-off.

CAREER HIGHLIGHTS

1934   US Masters
1936   US Masters

SMITH, MACDONALD (1890-1949)

Although probably the best of three Carnoustie-born golfing brothers, the others being Alex and Willie, he never managed to win a major championship despite coming close on several occasions. He tied for the US Open in 1910 but lost the play-off with Johnny McDermott and his own brother Alex, who became champion. He was second again in 1930 to Bobby Jones and in the top six on four other occasions.

In the British Open his record was even more incredible. He was second in 1930 (to Jones again) and in 1932, third in 1923 and 1924, fourth in 1925 and 1934 and fifth in 1931. He should have won in 1925 when he had a five-shot lead going into the final round at Prestwick, but he shot an 82. However, in a career that spanned over a quarter of a century, he enjoyed a successful tournament record, winning over 30 events in America between the wars.

CAREER HIGHLIGHTS

1926   Canadian Open

TAYLOR, J.H. (1871–1963)

In 1894 John Henry Taylor became the first English professional to win the Open. This was the first time the Championship was held outside Scotland, at Sandwich in Kent. A member of the Great Triumvirate, along with Harry Vardon and James Braid, he began his life as a golf professional at Burnham in Somerset. He was already by then an excellent player, and proved it the following year when he defeated Andrew Kirkcaldy in a match and shortly thereafter followed the Scot as professional at Winchester.

The 1895 Open was played at St Andrews. Taylor retained the trophy and was acclaimed as the finest player in Britain. A year later he met Harry Vardon for the first time in a head-to-head match, played at Ganton where Vardon was the professional. Taylor suffered a heavy defeat, going down 8 and 7. A month later they were battling against each other once again but on this occasion it was in a play-off for the Open Championship at Muirfield. Vardon was the victor.

In 1900 St Andrews was again the venue for Taylor's next Open victory, and this time he won emphatically, beating his main rival Harry Vardon by seven shots and becoming only the third

SNEAD, SAM (b 1912)

He is one of a small band of famous players whose illustrious careers contain one flaw: they missed out on one of the major championships. With Arnold Palmer it was the US PGA, with Lee Trevino it was the US Masters, and with Snead it was the US Open. He came extraordinarily close, finishing second on four occasions, and there were times when he could have expected to have won. In 1939 at Philadelphia, he took eight at the final hole when five would have been good enough. In 1947 he missed a comparatively short putt on the final hole of the play-off after a tie with Lew Worsham.

Despite these slips, he won both the Masters and the US PGA three times and the British Open once, in 1946 at St Andrews. Perhaps the stage for his greatest achievements was Augusta where, with Ben Hogan, he helped to establish the Masters as a prestige event. Between

1949 and 1954 he won three times and Hogan twice. His US PGA wins were all in match-play, in 1942, 1949 and 1951, a side of golf that seemed tailor-made for him. This is also well illustrated by his Ryder Cup record: in seven matches between 1937 and 1959 he was beaten only once, by Harry Weetman at Wentworth in 1953. On the US Tour he amassed 84 victories, substantially more than anyone else; closest to him is Nicklaus with 71.

CAREER HIGHLIGHTS

1938	Canadian Open
1940	Canadian Open
1941	Canadian Open
1942	US PGA
1946	The Open
1949	US Masters
	US PGA
1951	US PGA
1952	US Masters
1954	US Masters

man to break 80 in every round. Third place on that occasion went to James Braid.

Taylor took his fourth Open title at Deal in 1909; his final victory came at Hoylake in 1913 after he had had to hole a six-footer to qualify for the Championship proper. After that fifth Open win he began to decline as a major figure in the game although he was still good enough to play in the first Great Britain v America match in 1921; he was also a winning Ryder Cup captain in 1933. As a founder member of the PGA in 1901, he served as both chairman and captain.

CAREER HIGHLIGHTS

1894	The Open
1895	The Open
1900	The Open
1904	PGA Match-Play
1908	French Open
	PGA Match-Play
1909	The Open
	French Open
1913	The Open

THOMSON, PETER, CBE (b 1929)

By far the best Australian golfer until Greg Norman arrived on the scene in the 1980s, he won more British Opens than any golfer since Harry Vardon. His five Open titles came in 1954, 1955, 1956, 1958 and 1965; the three successive wins from 1954–56 equalled the record set by Tom Morris Junior.

Not renowned as a long hitter, his strengths were his chipping and putting allied to good long-iron play. His first tournament victory came in 1950 when he won the New Zealand Open, a feat he was to repeat a further seven times. His first visit to Britain was in 1951 when he finished a creditable sixth in the Open. The following year he was second behind South African Bobby Locke with whom he dominated the Championship in the 1950s.

He was encouraged to compete in America which he did successfully, winning the 1956 Texas Open, but he never seemed comfortable playing there. Some say it was because he preferred to play the small ball as opposed to the larger

1.68 ball used on the US Tour. However, in the same year as his win in Texas, he also finished four strokes behind Cary Middlecoff in the US Open and the following year was fifth in the US Masters.

Apart from his five Open Championship titles, he won 20 other events including the PGA Match-Play on four occasions, the Dunlop Masters twice and the Alcan Golfer of the Year. His success as a player stemmed from a simple basic swing and meticulous preparation in setting-up before playing a shot.

He announced his retirement from tournament golf in 1979 and since then he has been involved in broadcasting and writing for an Australian national newspaper. He has lately returned to play on the Seniors Tour with great success, ironically in America where he was less happy when at the height of his powers.

CAREER HIGHLIGHTS

1950	New Zealand Open
1951	Australian Open
	New Zealand Open
1953	New Zealand Open
1954	The Open
	PGA Match-Play
1955	The Open
	New Zealand Open
1956	The Open
1958	The Open
1959	New Zealand Open
	Italian Open
	Spanish Open
1960	Hong Kong Open
	German Open
	New Zealand Open
1961	PGA Match-Play
	New Zealand Open
1963	Indian Open
1964	Philippines Open
1965	The Open
	Hong Kong Open
	New Zealand Open
1966	PGA Match-Play
1967	PGA Match-Play
	Australian Open
	Hong Kong Open
1971	New Zealand Open
1972	Australian Open
1976	Indian Open

TREVINO, LEE (b 1939)

One of the great characters of the game, he mixes sparkling golf with constant chatter interspersed with a good line in jokes. Some say his banter and non-stop quips contain a generous slice of gamesmanship capable of distracting many an opponent. Others see his clowning as just part of the professional scene.

He learned the game the hard way, hustling for dollars in money matches. After four years in the Marines, he worked as an assistant in El Paso and managed to develop his game in between his duties in the pro shop. He joined the US tour in 1967 and a year later won the US Open as a virtual unknown, having finished 54th and sixth the previous two years. He won it again in 1971, beating Jack Nicklaus in a play-off at Merion.

By then he had truly arrived, and weeks later at Royal Birkdale he collected the Open Championship, becoming only the fourth player to have won both titles in the same year. When he went to Muirfield a year later to defend the crown, many felt that Tony Jacklin was in line for his second Open triumph. They were at the front of the field in the last round and things looked bright for Jacklin until Trevino holed a chip on the 71st hole to destroy the Englishman's hopes. 'Supermex', as he had become known, retained the title with Nicklaus in second spot.

He has never won the Masters, and feels that his game is not suited to the Augusta course, but he has collected two US PGA Championships in 1974 and 1984, the latter at the age of 44. In all he has won 27 US Tour events and many more worldwide, all this despite suffering frequent back trouble after being struck by lightning during the 1975 Western Open. He underwent surgery and continues to be among the best players in the world and a frequent visitor to Britain.

He has played in six Ryder Cup matches and was non-playing captain in 1985 at The Belfry, where he had the dubious distinction of seeing America lose their grip on the trophy after a spell of 28 years.

CAREER HIGHLIGHTS

1968	US Open
1971	The Open
	US Open
	Canadian Open
1972	The Open
1974	US PGA
1977	Canadian Open
1979	Canadian Open
1984	US PGA

VARDON, HARRY (1870–1937)

At the age of 20 he had played golf on no more than a couple of dozen occasions, but when he saw that his brother Tom was making money at the game he decided to follow suit. He was to become one of the legends of the game and win its highest achievement, the Open Championship, no

fewer than six times: in 1896, 1898, 1899, 1903, 1911 and 1914.

His first Open appearance was in 1893, when he made little impression, but the following year he finished in fifth place. A month before the 1896 Open at Muirfield, he played a challenge match with the current Open champion, J.H. Taylor. He won 8 and 7 and went on to win his first Open title, defeating Taylor in a play-off.

He had a great influence on the technical side of the game, especially in the method of gripping the club. He developed a way to compensate for the slimmer handles that became a feature of the hickory-shafted clubs which superseded the thicker, more cumbersome implements used previously. This method became known as the 'Vardon grip' and is still favoured by most of the top players today.

In 1900 he won the US Open, the climax of a year-long tour of exhibition matches in America. This tour no doubt contributed to the breakdown in his health which occurred in 1903, obliging him to spend many months in a sanatorium. Although he came back to

win other major championships, he never quite regained the form he showed at his peak between 1896 and 1903.

His great strength as a player was his accuracy, especially with fairway woods. It was even said that he had problems when playing a course twice in the same day because he always hit his ball into the divot holes made by his shots in the previous round! That story may be fiction, but it was nevertheless in recognition of his supreme accuracy that the award, presented each year to the player with the lowest stroke average, was named the Vardon Trophy after the great man.

CAREER HIGHLIGHTS

1896	The Open
1898	The Open
1899	The Open
1900	US Open
1903	The Open
1911	The Open
1912	PGA Match-Play
1914	The Open

VENTURI, KEN (b 1931)

When he commentates on the US Masters for one of America's main TV networks, he probably reflects on his own unfortunate memories of Augusta. In 1956, when still an amateur, he shot 66 and 69 to lead the field and despite a third-round 75 was still well placed going into the final round. With two holes left he still led but a bogey at the 17th proved his undoing; Jack Burke grabbed a birdie to win by one shot.

Four years later, and now a seasoned pro, he suffered again. After three rounds he trailed Arnold Palmer by one stroke but with two holes left he had turned that into a one-shot lead. Again it was not to be as Palmer birdied two of the last three holes to restore his one-stroke advantage and take the title.

He did, however, secure one major title, the US Open in 1964, despite trailing by six shots at halfway. A third-round 66 put him four ahead of Palmer and in the final round – 36-holes were then played on the final day – he held on despite heat problems to win.

In the early part of his professional career he was a frequent winner on the US Tour, being a noted iron player, but he lost consistency and his health began to suffer. This forced a premature end to his career in 1967 after 14 Tour wins.

CAREER HIGHLIGHTS

1964   US Open

VICENZO, ROBERTO DE (b 1923)

He has the unique distinction of being more famous for the tournament he lost than the many he won. In 1968 he stormed through the field in the final round of the US Masters with a brilliant closing score, seemingly to force a play-off with Bob Goalby. Unfortunately it was then discovered that he had signed his card for a 66 when in fact he had scored 65. Sadly the score he signed for had to stand and Goalby took the title.

One of the game's most popular players, he was born in Buenos Aires and is the finest golfer to emerge from South America. Despite many tournament wins all over the world his driving ambition was to win the British Open. Year after year he made the pilgrimage to Britain in

search of his personal 'Holy Grail', and although he came close on several occasions the years passed and it seemed his chance was gone. But he refused to give up and in 1967 at Hoylake, aged 44, he finally became Open Champion.

He won the Argentine Open nine times and collected more than 240 tournament victories worldwide. Seldom has there been a more popular golfer; he continues to attract a host of admirers when he appears on the Seniors Circuit.

CAREER HIGHLIGHTS

1944	Argentine Open
1946	Chile Open
1947	Colombian Open
1949	Argentine Open
	Uruguay Open
1950	Belgian Open
	French Open
	Dutch Open
1951	Argentine Open
	Mexican Open
1952	Argentine Open
	Panama Open
1953	Mexican Open
1956	Jamaican Open
1957	Jamaican Open
	Brazilian Open
1958	Argentine Open
1960	French Open
	Brazilian Open
1963	Brazilian Open
1964	French Open
	German Open
	Brazilian Open
1965	Argentine Open
1966	Spanish Open
1967	The Open
	Argentine Open
1970	Argentine Open
1973	Panama Open
	Brazilian Open
1974	Argentine Open
	Panama Open

WADKINS, LANNY (b 1949)

Like many of today's top American Tour players, he enjoyed a highly successful amateur career. He was only 16 when he finished high in the order in the US Amateur, and in 1970 he won it together with two other championships.

He played in the 1969 and 1971 Walker Cup matches, finished runner-up in the 1970 Heritage Classic and turned professional in 1971. In 1972 he won the Sahara Invitational and was 10th in the money list, which brought him the Rookie of the Year award.

His career has seen many peaks and troughs. Arguably his best year was 1977 when he won his only Major, the US PGA at Pebble Beach, beating Gene Littler in a play-off at the third extra hole.

He has also been runner-up twice, in 1982 and 1984, and in the 1986 US Open he came second behind Ray Floyd. He has been successful in Japan and Australia and has played in four Ryder Cup and three World Cup teams.

CAREER HIGHLIGHTS

1970	US Amateur
1977	US PGA
1978	Canadian Open

WATSON, TOM (b 1949)

In the nine years from 1975 to 1983 he stamped his presence on the major championships and dominated the game in America. When he arrived at Carnoustie in 1975 for the Open Championship he was just another young tour player, but a few days later his name was celebrated throughout the golfing world. He tied with Australia's Jack Newton after 72 holes and won the 18-hole play-off, since when he has chalked up four more British Opens, in 1977, 1980, 1982 and 1983, two US Masters in 1977 and 1981, and one US Open in 1982.

Several of those victories have been real thrillers, none more so than the 1977 Open at Turnberry when he survived a last-round shoot-out with Jack Nicklaus which reached a fitting climax on the final green. Nicklaus slotted in a long putt for a birdie which looked like securing a play-off until Watson followed him in to take the title with a 65 to Nicklaus's 66. It was a similar story in the 1982 US Open at Pebble Beach when he birdied the final two holes to pip Nicklaus, the crunch coming when he chipped in at the short 17th after looking set to take four. He again left Nicklaus as his victim in the 1977 Masters when, despite a typical final round of 66 from the Golden Bear, he completed a 67 to win by two shots.

Having won the Open again in 1982 at Troon and the following year at Birkdale, he went to St Andrews in 1984 seeking a hat-trick. He was tied with Seve Ballesteros when he reached the Road Hole 17th in the final round. But he overclubbed with his second, left the ball almost against the retaining wall and could only make bogey. That left him a shot behind, and then Ballesteros birdied the 18th and took the title.

So far the only Major that has eluded him is the US PGA, in which he was pipped in a play-off by John Mahaffey in 1978. He has topped the US money list five times, including four times in a row from 1977, and has played in three Ryder Cups. With eight Majors to his credit, Watson can certainly be called one of golf's great players.

CAREER HIGHLIGHTS

1975	The Open
1977	The Open
	US Masters
1980	The Open
1981	US Masters
1982	The Open
	US Open
1983	The Open

WETHERED, JOYCE – LADY HEATHCOAT-AMORY (b 1901)

She took up golf at the age of 17 during a family holiday in Scotland, encouraged by her brother Roger, one of the oustanding amateur players of that era. In 1920, aged 19, she entered the English Championship at Sheringham just, so she said, to keep a friend company. She did much more than that, she reached the final where she caused a major upset by defeating Cecil

Leitch, the finest lady golfer in the country.

Over the next four years she was virtually unbeatable, playing 33 matches and winning them all. Although she lost the 1921 British Amateur to Cecil Leitch, thereafter she had the upper hand in all their encounters. She retired from championship golf in 1925 but returned to compete at St Andrews in 1929, and in one of her finest performances beat the top American Glenna Collett by 3 and 1. This crowned a fabulous career and with nothing left to conquer or prove she, like her male counterpart Bobby Jones, finally retired at the very height of her powers.

CAREER HIGHLIGHTS

1922	British Ladies' Amateur
1924	British Ladies' Amateur
1925	British Ladies' Amateur
1929	British Ladies' Amateur

WOOD, CRAIG (1901–68)

Few players can have suffered more disappointments in major championships. A formidable player in the 1930s and early 1940s, he was nearly always the bridesmaid in the big events.

His chapter of woe began in 1933 when he was third in the US Open then lost a play-off for the British Open to Densmore Shute at St Andrews. The

following year he finished a shot behind Horton Smith in the US Masters then lost in the final of the US PGA to Paul Runyan. In 1935 he led the Masters by three shots going into the final round and, despite faltering, played the last eight holes four under par to look the likely winner. The cheque was even being prepared for him until Gene Sarazen had an albatross two at the 15th. Wood was so stunned that he lost the play-off by five shots over 36 holes.

Still the fates had not finished. In the 1939 US Open, he tied with Byron Nelson and Shute to force an 18-hole play-off. Shute was eliminated as Wood and

Nelson each shot 68. Out they went again only for Wood to be pipped as Nelson sank a full 1-iron.

His luck changed at last in the 1941 Masters when he took revenge on Nelson to win his first Major by three shots. That gave him an important boost and he went on to take the US Open that year. He was also a Ryder Cup player from 1931 to 1935.

CAREER HIGHLIGHTS

1941	US Open
	US Masters
1942	Canadian Open

ZAHARIAS, BABE (1914-56)

Probably one of the greatest sportswomen of all time. Born Mildred Didrikson, she became 'The Babe' when she won six out of seven track and field events before the 1932 Olympics. In the Games themselves she won the hurdles, javelin and high jump but was later deprived of the high-jump gold medal because her method of clearing the bar head-first was declared illegal. A natural at all games, she was proficient at basketball, baseball, tennis, diving, skating and bowling.

She switched to golf in the mid-1930s and with her remarkable power was soon a winner. After taking the Texas Open in 1935 she was declared a professional because she earned money from her other sports. Three years later she married wrestler George Zaharias and in 1940 she won the Texas Open and the Western Open but refused the prize-money. In 1943 she was reinstated as an amateur then in 1946 and 1947 she won 17 events in a row including the US Amateur and the British Women's at Gullane, accounting for Frances Stephens and Jean Donald on her way to a 5 and 4 victory against Jacqueline Gordon in the final. In 1948 Zaharias turned professional of her own accord, was a founder member of the ladies' pro tour and won the US Open at Atlantic City, one of three victories from eight events.

She won the US Open again in 1950 and the following year claimed seven wins as the tour expanded to 14 events. In 1953 she underwent an operation for

cancer but she was soon back on tour, winning five events the following year including the US Open by 12 strokes. She won twice more in 1955 but further operations followed until she lost her battle against the disease in 1956. In all she had 31 tournament wins.

CAREER HIGHLIGHTS

1946	US Ladies' Amateur
1947	British Ladies' Amateur
1948	US Women's Open
1950	US Women's Open
1954	US Women's Open

ZOELLER, FUZZY (b 1951)

Frank Urban Zoeller, nicknamed 'Fuzzy' because of his initials, is one of the game's blithe spirits believing that playing golf certainly beats working. He turned professional in 1974 but had to wait until 1979 for his first victory on the US Tour when he captured the San Diego Open. Two months later he found himself tied with Ed Sneed and Tom Watson in the first sudden-death play-off in the history of the US Masters. Zoeller took the title at his first attempt when he holed a birdie putt on the second extra hole.

From then on he became a regular winner and in 1984 elevated himself still further when he captured the US Open after a play-off with Greg Norman. His towel-waving gesture on the 72nd hole of Winged Foot in that Championship won him the hearts of millions. Troubled by a back injury sustained during a basketball game at school, he underwent surgery in late 1984 but has won four more titles since. His best year on the US Tour came in 1986 when he won over $350,000 and his career earnings now stand at over $2 million.

CAREER HIGHLIGHTS

| 1979 | US Masters |
| 1984 | US Open |

INDEX

Page numbers in italics refer to captions.

A

Aaron, T. 79
Adams, J. 69
Agnew, S. 117
Alcan Golfer of The Year 165
Alcott, A. 131
Alliss, P. 71, 118, 122, 122
Amateur Championship 13, 39, 41, 45, 46, 50, 61, 82, 95, 116, 104, 123, 125, 130, 134, 138, 140, 142
Anderson, J. 63
Anderson, R. 150
Anderson, W. 82, 87, 122, 122
Andy Williams San Diego Open 118
Aoki, I. 74, 96, 96, 122, 122
Archer, G. 79
Argentine Open 168
Armour, T. 35, 68, 91, 91, 123, 123
Atlanta Country Club 87, 93
Atlantic City 171
Auchterlonie, L. 25
Augusta National 50, 50, 52, 54, 56, 61, 77, 77, 79, 79, 80, 80, 130, 141, 155, 157, 163, 166
Australian Amateur Championship 147
Australian Open 158
Australian PGA Championship 151, 154
Ayton, D. 34

B

Bader, D. 118
Baker, K. 110
Baker-Finch, I. 74
Ball, J. 41, 41, 42, 63, 123, 123, 138
Ballesteros, S. 16, 34, 35, 38, 42, 45, 54, 72, 73, 73, 74, 80, 97, 97, 100, 103, 119, 124, 124, 139, 148, 149, 155, 169
Ballybunion 50
Baltusrol 57, 60, 85, 86, 87
Barber, J. 92
Barber, M. 112, 113
Barnes, J. 67, 68, 82, 91
Barton, P. 106, 125, 125
Baugh, L. 109
Bean, A. 74, 139
Beaconsfield 120
Belfry, The 124, 141, 166
Belgian Open 148
Bellerive 86
Benaud, R. 119, 120
Berg, P. 107
Berkshire Trophy 157
Berkshire, The 45, 46, 46, 66
Bing Crosby National Pro-Am 56, 116
Bob Hope Desert Classic 116, 141
Bolt, T. 84, 85, 128
Bonallack, M. 125, 125, 129
Boros, J. 84, 85, 86, 92, 112, 126, 126, 149
Boys' Championship 13, 125
Bradley, P. 110
Bradshaw, H. 46, 69, 69, 126, 127
Brae Burn 106
Braid, J. 16, 63, 64, 66, 127, 127, 128, 138, 160, 163, 164
Brazilian Open 130
Brewer, G. 79
British Assistants' Championship 122
British Ladies' Open Championship 110, 110
British Seniors' Open 114
British Women's Amateur Championship 104, 104, 105, 105, 107, 125, 170, 171
Brown, E. 42, 128, 128
Bruen, J. 45
Bucher, O. 112
Burke, B. 82
Burke, J. 78, 160, 166
Burke, K. 78
Burnham 163
Burns, G. 137
Burton, R. 69
Busson, H. 25
Butler, P. 95
Byrd, S. 153

C

Campbell, D. 125
Campbell, G. 118
Campbell, W. 82
Canadian Open 72, 157, 158
Carner, J. 110, 129, 129
Carnoustie 35, 35, 36, 36, 68, 69, 70, 72, 92, 123, 131, 139, 150, 169
Carr, J. 48, 129, 129
Casper, W. 57, 79, 85, 86, 114, 115, 130, 130, 143

D

Daks Tournament 122
Daly, F. 69, 132, 133, 161
Danielle, S. 120
Darnley, Lord 10, 16, 104
Darwin, B. 14

Cerda, A. 135
Champions 86
Chapman, R. 38
Charles 5th Earl of Elgin 11
Charles, R. 42, 70, 71, 96, 114, 130, 130.
Charlton, R. 119, 120
Chatto, T. 10
Chen, T. 88
Cherry Hills 85, 86, 87, 93, 137, 158
Coles, N. 16, 95, 95, 131, 131
Colgate Conglomerate 96
Colgate European Ladies' Championship 109, 110, 145
Colgate-Dinah Shore Winner's Circle 107
Collett, G. 105, 106, 106, 170
Colonial Country Club 135
Colt, H. 45, 48
Columbus 92
Compston, A. 42, 128
Congressional 86, 92
Connelly, I. 134
Connery, S. 118, 118, 119
Coody, C. 79
Cook, P. 120
Coombe Hill 119
Cooper, Harry 78, 162
Cooper, Henry 119, 120, 121
Corbett, R. 119, 121
Corcoran, F. 107
Cotton, H. 16, 36, 46, 47, 68, 68, 69, 91, 100, 118, 131, 131, 133, 153, 155
Country Club, The, Brookline 60, 82, 86, 86
Crampton, B. 113
Creavy, T. 91
Crenshaw, B. 80, 80, 92, 97, 99, 119, 132, 132, 137
Crosby, B. 56, 116, 116, 117, 118
Cruickshank, R. 91
Crump, G. 58
Cupit, J. 86
Curtis Cup 106, 106, 129, 145
Curtis, H. 106, 106
Curtis, M. 106, 106
Cypress Point 52, 55, 56, 56, 116

Davies, L. 110
Dayton 92
Dean Martin Tucson Open 118
Demaret, J. 78, 133, 133, 147
Devlin, B. 95, 95
Dexter, E. 119, 125
Diegel, L. 91, 160
Dod, L. 104
Doonican, V. 119, 120
Doral Eastern Open 137
Douglass, D. 113
Duncan, G. 47, 66, 66, 67
Duncan, T. 95
Dunlop Masters 46, 48, 127, 128, 130, 141, 165
Dunlop Southport Event 131
Dunn Bros 23
Dunn, T. 45
Dutch Open 124
Dutra, O. 85, 91
Dye, P. 60, 60

E

East of Ireland Amateur Championship 129
Edinburgh Golfers, Hon Company of 11, 12, 39, 63
Edinburgh Town Council 10
Edward VIII 16
Eglington, Earl of 63
Egyptian Match-Play Championship 158
Eisenhower Trophy 13
English Women's Championship 105, 107, 169
European Open 41, 122, 148
European Tour 121, 124, 131, 141, 145, 147, 155
Evans, C. 82, 82

F

Faldo, N. 74, 97, 97, 134, 134
Faulkner, M. 48, 69, 134, 135, 135, 139, 161
Fazio, G. 85
Ferguson, R. 63
Fernie, W. 63
Ferrier, J. 92
Finsterwald, D. 92
Fleck, J. 57, 85
Floyd, R. 80, 88, 92, 93, 103, 135, 168
Flushing Meadow 82
Ford, D. 78, 149
Ford, G. 119
Forgan, R. 23
Forsyth, B. 116, 118
Four Stars Nat.

Pro-Celebrity 121
Fowler, H. 66
Fownes, H. 57
French Open 148, 153
French Women's Amateur Championship 125
Funseth, R. 137
Furgol, E. 85

G

Ganton 44, 45, 163
Geiberger, A. 92, 92, 135, 158
George VI 16, 69
German Open 141
Ghezzi, V. 85, 92
Gleneagles 106, 106
Goalby, B. 79, 167
Goodman, J. 82, 142
Goodrich Rubber Company 19
Gordon, J. 171
Gourlay, W. & J. 18
Graham, D. 87, 87, 92, 96, 136, 137, 139
Graham, L. 87
Grant, D. 56
Greater Greensboro Open 145
Greater Jacksonville Open 137
Green, H. 80, 87, 93, 137, 137
Guldahl, R. 53, 78, 85, 153
Gullane 104, 171

H

Hagen, W. 16, 46, 47, 66, 67, 82, 91, 91, 93, 105, 138, 138, 153, 161, 162
Hamilton, R. 92
Harmon, C. 78, 149
Harper, C. 92
Haskell, C. 19
Havers, A. 67, 138
Hawaiian Open 122
Hawkstone Park 145
Hayes, M. 74
Hazeltine National 86, 139, 160
Heafner, C. 149
Heathcoat-Amory, Lady (See Wethered, J.)
Hebert, L. 92
Henning, H. 114, 158
Herd, A. 19, 66
Hill, D. 87
Hilton, H. 41, 42, 63, 138, 138
Hoad, L. 119
Hogan, B. 36, 39, 54, 57, 58, 59, 61, 69, 78, 78, 82, 85, 86, 87, 92, 122, 130, 133, 139, 139, 149, 153, 154, 158, 163
Hollinwell 155

Hope, B. 116, 117, 117, 118
Horne, R. 132
Houston Invitational 144
Hoylake 20, 41, 41, 42, 63, 64, 65, 67, 68, 69, 70, 113, 123, 132, 138, 162, 164, 168
Hoyt, B. 106
Huan, L. 45, 72
Hunt, J. 119, 120
Hutchison, J. 66, 66, 91, 160
Hyndman, W. 34

I

Interlachen 82
Inverness, Ohio 39, 82, 87, 93, 139, 160
Irish Open 48, 127, 130, 132
Irish Professional Championship 132
Irwin, H. 74, 87, 96, 137, 139, 139
Italian Open 122, 130

J

Jacklin, A. 40, 42, 45, 47, 70, 71, 72, 74, 82, 86, 87, 96, 101, 118, 119, 130, 139, 140, 145, 160, 166
Jacobs, J. 102, 103
Jacobs, T. 79
James II 10
January, D. 92, 112, 113
John Player Classic 38, 130, 155
Jones, R. 16, 30, 32, 42, 42, 45, 50, 52, 54, 57, 59, 61, 66, 67, 67, 77, 79, 80, 82, 85, 87, 92, 105, 106, 122, 123, 138, 140, 140, 153, 162, 170
Jurado, J. 35, 36

K

Keiser, H. 78
Kent Open 131
Kentucky Derby Open 158
Kidd, T. 63
Killarney 50
Kincaid, T. 22, 26
Kirkcaldy, A. 163
Kite, T. 80

L

Lacoste, C. 125
Ladies' Golf Union 104, 107
Ladies' Professional

Golfers' Asc. 107, 109
Lahinch 48, 48, 50
Lancaster, B. 119
Lancome Trophy 130, 150
Landale, W. 12
Langer, B. 53, 74, 80, 97, 98, 140, 141, 141, 145
Laurel Valley 92
Leadbetter, D. 134
Legends Of Golf, The 112
Leitch, C. 104, 105, 105, 170
Leith 11
Lema, T. 70, 95, 141, 141, 158
Lemmon, J. 119
Leno, D. 116
Lithgoe, E. 104
Little, L. 84, 85, 142, 142, 162
Littler, G. 79, 86, 92, 96, 114, 130, 143, 143, 168
Locke, A. 32, 46, 69, 69, 70, 102, 127, 133, 143, 144, 164
London Scottish Ladies' Club 104
Longhurst, H. 50
Lopez, N. 109, 109, 144, 144
Los Angeles Open 133, 139
LPGA Tour 107, 109, 110, 114, 129, 145
Lyle, A. 145
Lyle, S. 47, 74, 74, 97, 98, 98, 145, 145

M

Mackenzie, A. 52, 56
Mackenzie, K. 13, 13
Mahaffey, J. 87, 92, 158, 169
Maiden, S. 30, 106
Manero, T. 85
Mangrum, L. 84, 85, 133, 146, 147, 149
Mann, C. 107
Marr, D. 92
Marsh, D. 34
Marsh, G. 95, 96, 97, 101, 147, 148
Marsh, R. 147
Martini Tournament 154, 161
Mary, Queen of Scots 10, 16, 104
Massy, A. 65, 65, 73, 148, 148
Mathis, J. 119, 121
Matthews, Sir S. 114
Mature, V. 121
Mayer, R. 85, 133
McDermott, J. 82, 82, 162
McEwan 23
McGimpsey, G. 39

Medinah 60, 87
Memphis Classic 135
Merion 59, 59, 60, 85, 87, 87, 137, 165
Merrell, H. 56
Mexican Open 130
Middlecoff, C. 78, 85, 133, 149, 149, 165
Miller, J. 45, 57, 72, 79, 87, 99, 118, 119, 124, 149, 150
Mills, Sir W. 25
Minoprio, G. 107
Mitchell, A. 160
Mize, L. 77
Montgomerie, W. 18
Moody, O. 86
Morris, T. Junior 16, 23, 62, 63, 63, 150, 150, 151, 164
Morris, T. Senior 16, 39, 62, 62, 150, 151, 151, 161
Motor City Open 149
Muirfield 39, 39, 40, 40, 41, 63, 68, 69, 70, 71, 72, 72, 96, 106, 122, 131, 133, 134, 138, 140, 148, 153, 158, 163, 166
Musselburgh 63, 104

N

Nagle, K. 70, 86, 130, 151, 151, 157
Nakajima, T. 34, 54, 98, 98
National, The 60
Nelson, B. 53, 54, 78, 78, 85, 92, 130, 133, 152, 152, 170, 171
Nelson, L. 88, 88, 93
Neumann, L. 110
Neville, J. 56
New Mexico Women's Amateur Championship 109, 144
New Zealand Open 130, 151, 164
Newport 82
Newton, J. 36, 72, 169
Nichols, R. 92
Nicklaus, J. 16, 34, 36, 39, 42, 45, 54, 56, 57, 58, 59, 61, 70, 71, 72, 72, 73, 79, 79, 80, 81, 82, 86, 86, 87, 88, 92, 93, 95, 95, 96, 96, 98, 99, 100, 112, 114, 120, 122, 124, 130, 132, 135, 138, 139, 140, 141, 152, 153, 153, 155, 157, 158, 161, 163, 165, 166, 169
Nigerian Open 145
Norman, G. 16, 61, 74, 74, 80, 88, 88, 93, 97, 97, 98, 100, 110,

154, 154, 164, 172
North, A. 87, 88, 90

O

O'Connor, C. Senior 20, 42, 48, 50, 130, 155, 155
Oak Hill 39, 60, 86, 93
Oakland Hills 60, 85, 88, 92, 93
Oakmont Country Club 57, 57, 58, 85, 86, 87, 92, 149, 158
Olazabal, J-M. 98
Oliver, E. 92
Olympic 56, 57, 85, 86
Oosterhuis, P. 73, 79, 118, 119, 156, 157
Open Championship 10, 12, 13, 14, 16, 19, 20, 21, 32, 34, 35, 36, 36, 38, 38, 40, 41, 43, 45, 46, 47, 47, 48, 50, 61, 62-76, 62, 64, 65, 66, 67, 68, 69, 71, 73, 74, 80, 91, 92, 95, 96, 105, 112, 113, 118, 122, 123, 126, 127, 128, 130, 131, 132, 133, 134, 135, 137, 138, 140, 141, 143, 145, 147, 148, 149, 150, 157, 158, 160, 161, 162, 163, 164, 165, 166, 167, 168, 169, 170
Ouimet, F. 82, 82, 86
Owen, S. 73
Owens, C. 113, 114

P

Padgham, A. 68, 69
Palmer, A. 13, 42, 45, 54, 57, 57, 58, 70, 72, 79, 79, 85, 86, 92, 95, 95, 96, 102, 112, 117, 119, 122, 130, 151, 152, 153, 157, 157, 158, 163, 166
Park, M. 63
Park, W. 23, 45, 62, 62, 150, 151
Pate, J. 56, 87, 92, 158, 158
Patrick 23
Patton, W. 78
Pearson, I. 104
Pebble Beach 54, 55, 56, 87, 88, 88, 92, 116, 168, 169
Pecan Valley 92
Peers, D. 118
Pelham 91
Penfold Tournament 131
Perry, A. 68, 68
Petron 30
PGA Championship 134, 140, 158

PGA West 60
Philadelphia 153, 163
Philp, H. 23
Picard, H. 78, 92
Pine Valley 58, 58, 59
Pinehurst 39, 60
Platt, W. 58
Player, G. 36, 54, 61, 70, 72, 79, 80, 80, 86, 92, 93, 93, 95, 96, 96, 99, 102, 112, 113, 116, 119, 137, 139, 141, 152, 154, 158, 159, 160
Portmarnock 48, 48, 130
Portuguese Open 122, 135
Prairie Dunes 106
Prestwick 12, 36, 36, 62, 63, 65, 67, 68, 142, 150
Price, N. 54, 74, 147
Prince's, Sandwich 68, 106, 161
Professional Golfers' Association 20, 110, 164

Q

Queen Adelaide Gold Medal 12

R

Rawlins, H. 82
Rawls, B. 107
Ray, T. 82, 118, 139, 148, 160, 160
Rees, D. 45, 70, 160, 160
Revolta, J. 91
Richardson, R. 104
Riviera 85, 93
Robertson, A. 62, 151, 161, 161
Rodgers, P. 70, 71
Rodriguez, C. 114, 115
Rogers, W 34, 74, 96, 97, 141
Romford 128
Rosberg, R. 92
Ross, D. 39
Royal and Ancient Golf Club 12, 13, 13, 14, 15, 16, 18, 19, 20, 21, 24, 24, 25, 38, 63, 66, 126
Royal Birkdale 13, 42, 43, 45, 70, 72, 72, 74, 110, 124, 128, 139, 149, 153, 157, 158, 160, 166, 169
Royal County Down 48
Royal Dornoch 39
Royal Liverpool (see Hoylake) 41
Royal Lytham and St Annes 41, 42, 42, 43, 67, 67, 69, 70, 71, 72, 73, 73, 104,

113, 124, 130, 139, 140, 142, 148, 155
Royal Melbourne 56
Royal Portrush 48, 48, 69, 104, 135
Royal St George's 34, 46, 47, 63, 65, 66, 68, 68, 69, 73, 74, 74, 82, 126, 131, 138, 141, 145, 148, 163
Royal Troon 36, 37, 38, 67, 67, 69, 70, 72, 74, 105, 133, 138, 152, 157, 161, 169
Ruiz, L. 42
Runyan, P. 91, 92, 170
Ryder Cup 36, 45, 69, 106, 114, 122, 124, 126, 128, 130, 131, 133, 135, 137, 139, 140, 141, 145, 147, 149, 150, 153, 154, 155, 158, 160, 161, 162, 163, 164, 166, 168, 169, 171

S

Sahara Invitational 168
Sammy Davis Greater Hartford Open 118
San Diego Open 143, 172
Sanders, D. 72, 72, 114, 115, 117
Sarazen, G. 32, 38, 52, 54, 61, 68, 77, 77, 82, 82, 86, 91, 91, 95, 105, 139, 142, 154, 158, 161, 161, 162, 170
Saunton 66
Savalas, T. 119, 119, 120
Scioto 39
Scott, Hon M. 104
Scott, Lady M. 104, 104, 106
Scottish Amateur Championship 128
Sea Pines Heritage Classic 134, 137, 139, 141, 147, 168
Secombe, Sir H. 118
Seminole 39
Seniors' Championship 13, 155
Sheringham 105
Shinnecock Hills 60, 60, 88
Shoal Creek 93, 93
Shute, D. 32, 68, 85, 91, 91, 153, 170
Smith, A. 82, 162
Smith, H. 52, 52, 77, 78, 80, 162, 162, 170
Smith, M. 36, 68, 82, 162, 162
Smith, W. 162
Snead, S. 54, 69, 78, 85, 92, 103, 117, 130, 139, 149, 153,

154, 163, 163
Sneed, E. 80, 80, 172
Southern Hills 60, 87, 92, 93, 137
Spanish Open 122, 134, 135, 148, 158
Spring Mill 85
Spyglass Hill 116
St Andrews 9, 10, 10, 12, 14, 15, 15, 16, 16, 31, 31, 32, 32, 34, 35, 50, 62, 63, 66, 66, 67, 67, 68, 69, 70, 71, 72, 74, 92, 113, 113, 124, 125, 126, 130, 140, 141, 143, 148, 151, 153, 157, 161, 163, 169, 170
St Andrews Golfers, Society of 11, 12
St Andrews, New York 82
St Louis 85, 128
Stadler, C. 80
Stage Golfing Society 116
Stephenson, J. 109
Stewart, J. 119
Stirling, A. 106
Stockton, D. 92
Stranahan, F. 132, 133
Strange, C. 53, 53, 80
Strath, A. 62
Sun City $1 Million Challenge 135
Sunningdale 44, 45, 65, 109, 110, 145
Suntory 97
Sutton, H. 93
Swallow Penfold Championship 155
Swiss Open 128
Sykes, E. 120

T

Tait, F. 95
Tarbuck, J. 118, 119, 121
Taylor, J. 16, 46, 63, 64, 66, 82, 127, 128, 148, 163, 163, 166
Temple 118
Texas Open 106, 107, 113, 132, 164, 171
Texas PGA Championship 133
Thomas, D. 70, 71
Thomson, P. 32, 42, 45, 69, 70, 71, 95, 96, 112, 113, 143, 151, 153, 160, 164, 164
Thorburn, C. 120
Thoughts on Golve 22, 26
Tissies, H. 38
Tolley, C. 142
Torrance, S. 100
Tournament Players' Championship 145
Tournaments Players'

Club 60
TPC *60*
Travers, J. 82
Travis, W. 19
Trevino, L. 40, 45, 59, 72, *72*, 86, 87, 92, *93*, *93*, 96, 100, 101, 114, 119, 140, 165, *165*
True Temper *30*
Turnberry 36, 38, *38*, 72, *73*, 74, *74*, 114, 118, 155, 169
Turnesa, M. 92
Tway, R. 93, *93*, 155
Tweddell, Dr W. 142

U

U.S. Amateur Championship 19
Union Club 12
United States Golf Association 13, 20, 24, 87, 88, 91
US Amateur Championship 41, 57, 58, 59, 61, 80, 82, 130, 138, 140, 142, 143, 153, 157, 158
US Girls' Junior 129
US Masters 50, 52, *52*,

53, *53*, 54, 61, 77-81, *78*, *80*, *81*, 86, 88, 91, 95, 101, 124, 130, 132, 133, 135, 139, 140, 141, 142, 143, 144, 147, 149, 152, 153, 157, 158, 161, 162, 163, 165, 166, 167, 169, 170, 171, 172
US Open 56, 57, 58, 59, 61, 70, 72, 82-90, *82*, *84*, *86*, 87, 91, 92, 101, 118, 122, 123, 126, 130, 133, 135, 137, 138, 139, 140, 141, 142, 143, 147, 149, 152, 153, 155, 158, 160, 161, 162, 163, 165, 166, 168, 169, 170, 171, 172
US PGA 61, 88, 91-94, *91*, *92*, *93*, 112, 123, 126, 128, 130, 131, 133, 135, 137, 138, 139, 143, 149, 153, 155, 158, 160, 161, 163, 165, 166, 168, 169, 170
US PGA Seniors' Championship 126
US Senior Tour 112, 113, *113*, 114, 130, 143,

!55, 158, 160, 165, 168
US Tour 112, 113, 114, 116, 124, 126, 130, 132, 133, 135, 137, 139, 141, 143, 145, 147, 149, 154, 155, 157, 163, 165, 166, 167, 172
US Women's Amateur Championship 106, 107, 109, 110, 125, 129, 171
US Women's Open 107, *110*, 129, 171

V

Van Wie, V. 106
Vardon Trophy 66, 122, 133, 157, 166
Vardon, H. 16, 26, 45, 63, 65, *65*, 74, 82, 123, 127, 128, 148, 160, 161, 163, 164, 166, *166*
Vare Trophy 129
Vare, E. (See Collett, G.)
Venturi, K. 78, 86, *86*, 95, 100, 166, *167*
Vicenzo, R. de 42, 70, 79, 112, 151, 167,

167
Vickers, N. 112
Volpe, R. 109
Von Elm, G. 82

W

Wadkins, L. 92, 143, 168
Walker Cup 13, 34, 38, 41, 58, 106, 123, 125, 130, 142, 145, 157, 158, 168
Walker, M. 110, *110*
Wall, A. 79
Wallace, J. 142
Walton Heath 45, 46, 66, *91*, 128, 141
Wannsee Club 122
Waterville 50
Watrous, A. 42, 67, 91
Watson, T. 16, 34, 35, *35*, 36, 40, 45, 50, 54, 56, 72, *73*, 74, 80, *80*, 87, 88, *88*, 92, 101, 103, 112, 137, 139, 153, 158, 169, *169*, 172
Weetman, H. 163
Weiskopf, T. 53, 57, 72, 79, 96, 119, 158
Wentworth 20, 45, *46*, 62, 86, 95, 106,

119, 123, 124, 137, 139, 163
West Lake Classic 154
Western Open 91, 122, 166, 171
Westward Ho! 41, 104, 107
Wethered, J. 105, *105*, 169, *170*
Wethered, R. 66, 105, 142, 169
Wheaton 82
Whitcombe, E. 160
Whitcombe, R. 69
White, J. 65
William IV 12
Willock, H. *104*
Wilson, H. 59
Wilson, J. 23
Wimbledon Ladies' Club 104
Winchester 163
Winged Foot 60, 87, 88, *88*, 139, 172
Wogan, T. 119, 121, *121*
Women's Professional Golfers' Asc. 107, 110
Wood Collection, The *23*
Wood, C. 32, 52, 68, 77, 78, 85, 91, 153, 161, 170, *170*
Woodhall Spa 45

Work, B. 19
World Amateur Team Championship 158
World Cup 133, 151, 154, 168
World Match-Play Championship 46, 62, *86*, 95-98, *95*, 96, 97, 101, 122, *124*, 130, 137, 139, 141, 148, 154, 155, 158
Worsham, L. 85, 163
Wright, M. 107

Y

Young Professionals' Championship 157
Young, Prof D. 9
Youths' Championship 13

Z

Zaharias, M. 106, *106*, 107, 171, *171*
Zandvoort 124
Zembriski, W. 113, 114
Zoeller, F. 80, 88, *88*, 101, 119, 172, *172*

ACKNOWLEDGEMENTS

Acme Newspictures 125a, 167b
Associated Press 42, 72a
Barratts 155
BBC Hulton Picture Library 9, 11, 12, 15, 36, 47, 52, 64a & b, 65a & b, 66b, 67a, b & c, 68a, b, c & d, 83b & d, 84a, 92b, 105b, 106b, 123a, 131b, 138a & b, 150b, 161a, 162b, 163b

Alex Cowper 128
Bill Cox 151b
Peter Dazeley 21, 166
Dunlop 17, 20, 127a
Fotografia 118a
Frank Gardner 164
Golf Illustrated 27a, b, c & d, 28a, b, c & d, 29a, b, c, d, e & f, 30a & b, 41, 43, 62a & b, 66a, 71c, 83a, 91a, 105c, 106a & c, 116, 117, 122b, 127b, 151a, 163a,

The Publishers would like to thank the following sources for their help in providing the illustrations. (Where there is more than one

170a, 171
James Holden 22
International News Photos 71a, 78b

illustration on a page, the credits start with the picture furthest to the left and nearest the top of the page and work down each column.)

Stewart Kendall 90
National Museum of Antiquities 18, 104
Bert Neale Collection

71e, 84b, 126, 129b, 131a, 135a & c, 139a, 144c, 146, 152, 167a
New York Times 110, 148b
The Photo Source 24, 71d, f & g, 72b, 86a, 87, 118b, 122a, 133b, 140b, 149, 162a
Planet News 84d, 161b
Press Association 72c, 92, 95a, 118c, 133c

Phil Sheldon 60, 77b, 96b
Sport & General 95b, 96a, 130b, 157
Topical Press 123b, 142
United Press 84c
UPI 78a, 79, 86b, 141b, 143
Universal Pictorial Press 130a

The diagrams on pages 99-103 are by Phil Nunan.